Secrets from a Headhunter

LinkedIn Secrets for

Pharmaceutical

& Biotechnology Professionals

By:

Shanna Landolt

Table Of Contents

Table Of Contents

Secrets From a Headhunter:
LinkedIn Secrets for
Pharmaceutical & Biotechnology Professionals

Introduction

Welcome to Secrets From a Headhunter: LinkedIn Secrets for Pharmaceutical and Biotechnology Professionals. My promise is to provide you with the information that you need in order to show up in the top search results on LinkedIn as searched by recruiters, HR professionals and hiring managers in your geographical market and area of expertise. I will also walk you through how to use LinkedIn in a targeted job search.

The ultimate goal here is to create a great, professional looking; SEO optimized LinkedIn Profile so that you hear about the opportunities that are most appropriate for your career. As an added bonus, if you do everything I say here, you will also rank well in Google Search.

As a top executive recruiter and President of The Landolt Group www.landoltgroup.com and President of Secrets From a Headhunter www.secretsfromaheadhunter.com, I have worked with thousands of people in their job searches and have placed hundreds of people in six-figure jobs. I've had the privilege of being featured as a LinkedIn and job search expert on NBC, ABC, CBS, FOX and CityTV.

80% of jobs don't come through a recruiter, they come through networking — and LinkedIn is the largest business network in the world. There are now more than 300 million LinkedIn users with 2 new LinkedIn profiles being added every second. [1]

Even if you aren't *actively* in a job search, wouldn't you want to at least hear about great opportunities? That way you have the power of choice. You have 100% control: You can say "Yes" or "No."

One of the mistakes people make is to think of LinkedIn as the

1

equivalent of a snapshot of their resume. They miss the point that LinkedIn has become the online expression of their personal brand. Think about it, if you have a business meeting with someone, what is the first thing you do? You go on LinkedIn and look them up! And what's the next thing you do? You go on Google and see what else you can find. And, what you usually find in your Google search is their LinkedIn profile.

I wrote this book because, frankly, most of the LinkedIn profiles I see are awful! The more senior the person, the worse their LinkedIn profile usually is. And the bottom line is this: A weak profile is not going to produce the results you want.

If you're a normal human being, you probably have no idea how Search Engine Optimization (SEO) works when it comes to LinkedIn and how creating an optimized profile will allow for you to be in the top search results for your keywords and area of expertise. Follow the steps laid out in this book and I guarantee that SEO will work for you rather than against you.

The same goes for LinkedIn's Relevance Algorithm. Without taking this into consideration, you can fill out most of your LinkedIn Profile and still not come up to the top of search results because you don't have the right keywords in the right places. The tips I will provide you with will fix that.

Look, I get it. You're busy working and producing results for your company. You know that LinkedIn is important, and it's been on your to-do list, but then things come up and it slips into the "important, but not urgent" category.

Here's the problem. The employment market in the pharmaceutical and biotechnology industry has changed. Every month there are rumours of new mergers and acquisitions.

Product pipelines are thin. People are no longer spending the majority of their careers with one or two companies. Most importantly, people often don't have a choice about leaving an organization. How many rounds of cutbacks or layoffs have you heard about lately? And it's not just the poor performers who are being let go. Often your personal performance has nothing to do with being restructured out of a job.

I invite you to consider that EVERY job today is TEMPORARY. You will be in that job until either you choose to leave or you get packaged out. And if every job today is temporary, it's definitely in your interest to invest the time and care in developing your network, so that when the inevitable happens and you find yourself looking for work, you can be in the best possible position.

Here's what some of my clients have said about my Secrets From a Headhunter LinkedIn approach:

"I cannot recommend Shanna highly enough! She is extremely knowledgeable about the inner workings of LinkedIn, and different candidate search criteria for employers and perspective employees. She took the time to completely understand my situation, and made many recommendations for changes in my profile. In fact, after only making the first and simplest of her recommended changes, I was immediately contacted for a very senior role, consistent with my background. This was something that had not happened in several months, and I believe this was due to her recommendations giving me a higher profile for searches within LinkedIn." - Pharmaceutical Industry Senior Executive

"Shanna understands exactly how the search criteria operate, and can propose many changes to improve one's visibility. She knows specific SEO techniques, which would help even the most experienced LinkedIn user. She is also very technically savvy, and taught me things to more optimally use Skype in addition to LinkedIn." - Pharmaceutical Industry Senior Executive

"Shanna knows her stuff as a LinkedIn Expert. Most importantly, she gets how LinkedIn's Relevance Algorithm works. She understood what keywords were important to getting my profile higher in the rankings. She also recommended including video in my profile. Not only did this improve my LinkedIn profile, but it got my profile on the first page of Google for my search criteria. It's not an accident that NBC, FOX, ABC, CBS and City TV have turned to her for her expertise! On top of all of that she's professional, quick to respond, and great to work with." - Biotechnology Industry Senior Executive.

I first started using LinkedIn in 2008. My initial interactions with LinkedIn were just like everyone else. I felt my way through making my profile mostly by intuition. And because LinkedIn is very intuitive, it was fairly easy. However, I had no understanding of what made a good profile or a bad profile. When I look back, I'm now embarrassed about all of the important things I left out.

A few years ago I took on mastering LinkedIn. I decided to really grow my network. After a few months of sending out invitations to people, I had more than 5 people report that they didn't know me and LinkedIn shut down some of my privileges! How embarrassing!

I finally got serious and started to read everything I could find about LinkedIn. I Googled all the experts and purchased their training programs. I signed up for a Google Alert so that I got notified for every article about LinkedIn on the Internet. I kept reading book after book about LinkedIn. Then I took all of that knowledge, combined it with my insider knowledge as a headhunter and developed Secrets From a Headhunter: LinkedIn.

It's one thing to know LinkedIn. It's another thing to be able to get into the mind of a headhunter or executive recruiter and set up your profile so that recruiters and human resources professionals can contact you whenever they have something that could be a good fit. And again, even if you aren't actively in a job search right now, you want these people in your network because there will come a time when you will be and that's exactly the wrong time to have to build your profile up from scratch.

Here are a couple of myths my approach will clear up and overcome:

Myth: LinkedIn is only a piece of the puzzle. When I get in front of an interviewer, then I can show my stuff.

Secret from a Headhunter: LinkedIn is the #1 most important resource in your job search. Not having a great LinkedIn Profile will mean that you won't even hear about jobs in the hidden job market. You won't have the opportunity to show your stuff or get to the table.

Myth: As long as I have my job titles and companies on my profile, that should be good enough.

Secret from a Headhunter: LinkedIn ranks a "Complete Profile" as one of the most important criteria in their Relevance Algorithm. Not having a complete profile is a huge mistake and will drop you lower in the search rankings.

Myth: My job titles should be the same as on my resume.

Secret from a Headhunter: LinkedIn is a Profile and not a resume. You should put multiple appropriate titles for each role to get the best search results. This is a keyword strategy approach.

Myth: People are willing to look beyond my LinkedIn Profile.

Linked Insider Secret: Both recruiters as well as HR professionals often reject a candidate immediately based on a poor LinkedIn profile.

Myth: I don't need to have media clips or video on my profile.

Secret from a Headhunter: Media clips and video will pull your LinkedIn Profile higher on a Google Ranking. They will make you stand out.

Myth: Only connect with people that you know and trust.

Secret from a Headhunter: Connect with EVERYONE who works in your industry AND connect with people outside of your industry that seem credible.

Myth: It's fine to use a photo taken by a friend.

Secret from a Headhunter: Professionally taken photos are best. They are inexpensive and will help you stand out.

Myth: I should only connect with the recruiters I have worked with.

Secret from a Headhunter: Connect with every recruiter in your geographic area who specializes in your industry. Recruiters have some of the largest networks. Even if you don't use their services, it is in your personal interest to be connected to them.

Odds are you're a busy professional. I'll assume that you already have a LinkedIn profile. This book will walk you step-by-step through how to optimize your profile so you are in the top search results. Your profile will be compelling, and you will have an increased number of recruiters, HR professionals and hiring authorities reaching out to you.

I've designed each chapter so that you can update your profile one area at a time. Don't worry about having to do it all at once. If you take just 10-15 minutes a day, you will be in great shape in about a week.

Chapter 1
Start By Changing Your Settings.

We are going to start by changing the Privacy settings on your LinkedIn profile. This is a small step with big impact: Given that you are going to be making a number of changes to your profile, you do NOT want to notify your entire network of every single change you make, even if you are in an active job search. Having 20 updates in a matter of days won't look professional.

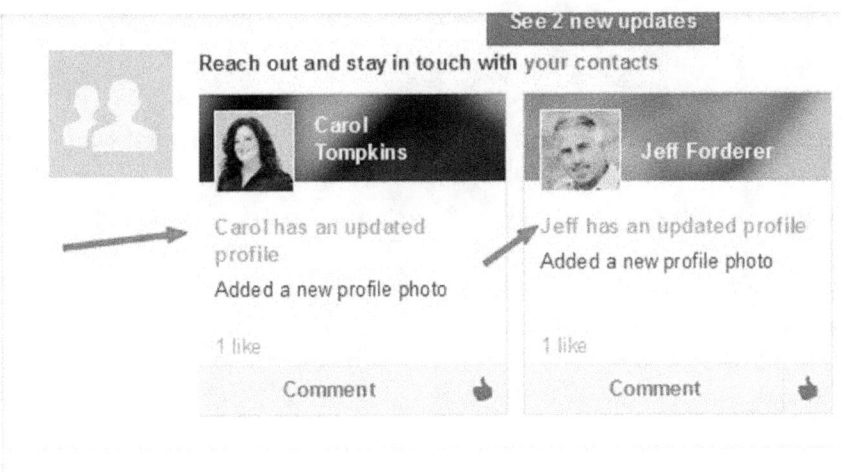

Step #1: Go to your **Privacy and Settings** Area. You will find it on the drop down menu under your small photo on the top right hand side of your profile.

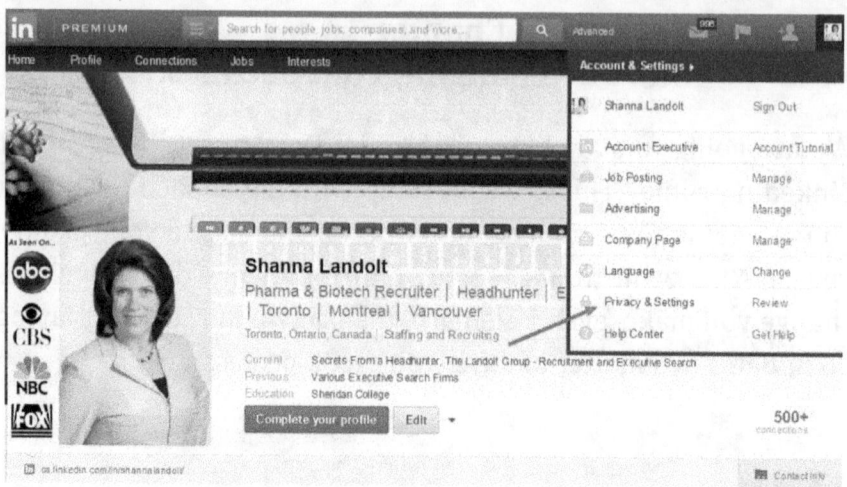

Step #2: Choose **Turn on/off your activity broadcasts**.

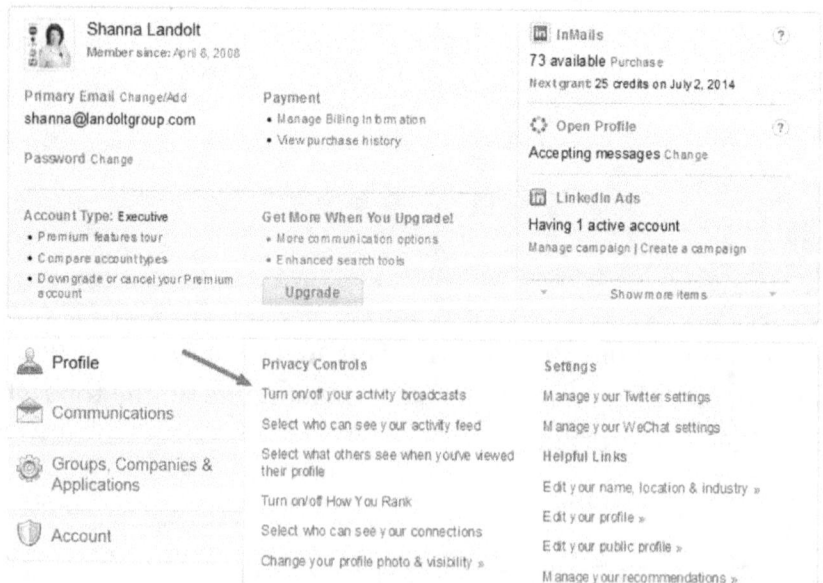

Step #3: Uncheck the box **Let people know when you change your profile, make recommendations, or follow companies** and then save changes.

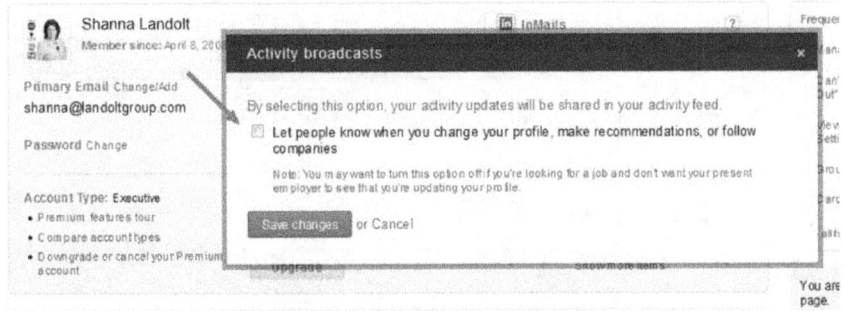

Step #4: In the same **Privacy and Settings** area choose **Select who can see your activity feed**.

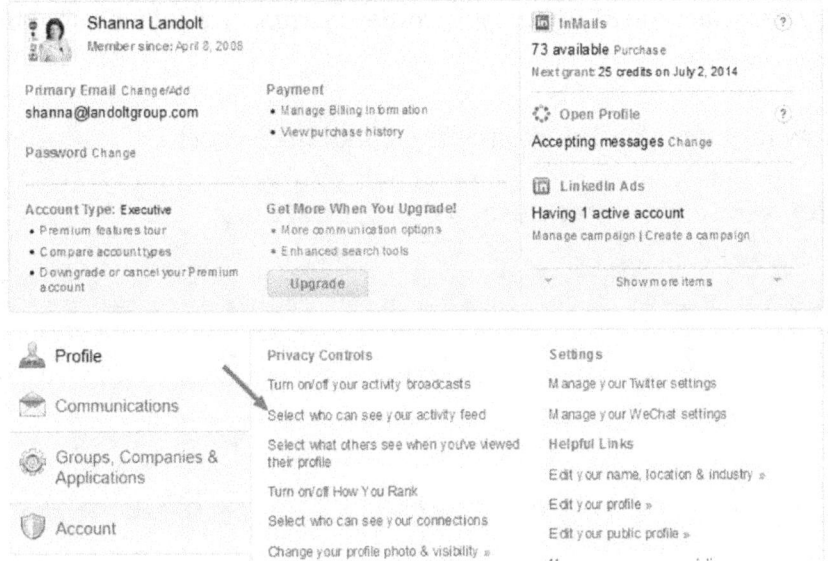

Step #5: Choose **Only you** on the drop down menu and save changes.

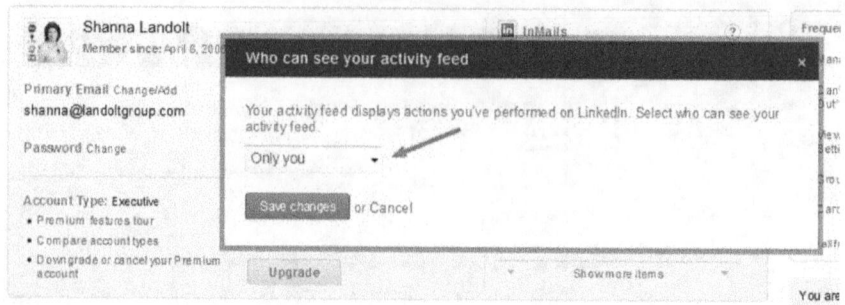

Your LinkedIn Profile settings are now in a mode where you will be able to make a number of changes to your profile without letting your entire network know. You can change these settings back later once the profile changes we will be making are complete.

Now for one of our more stealthy LinkedIn Secrets...

Step #6: Select **who can see your connections**.

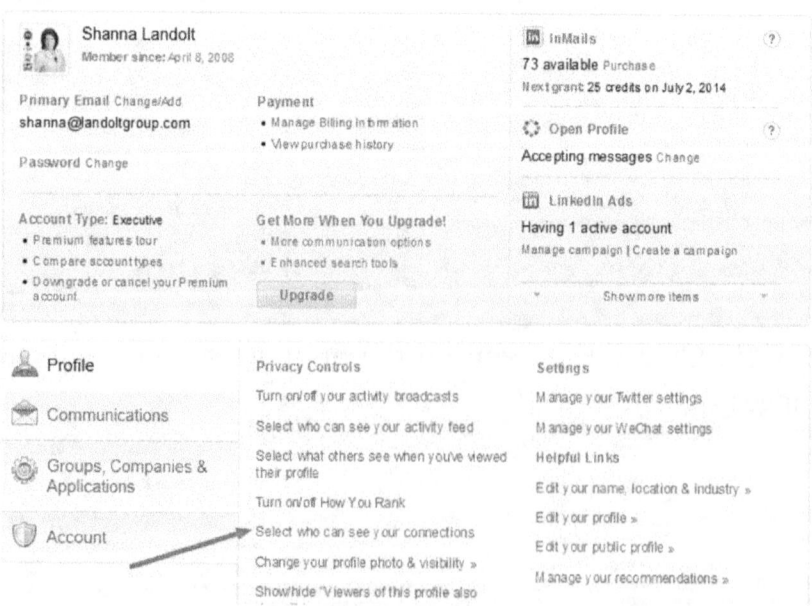

Step #7: Select **Only You** on the drop down menu and then save changes.

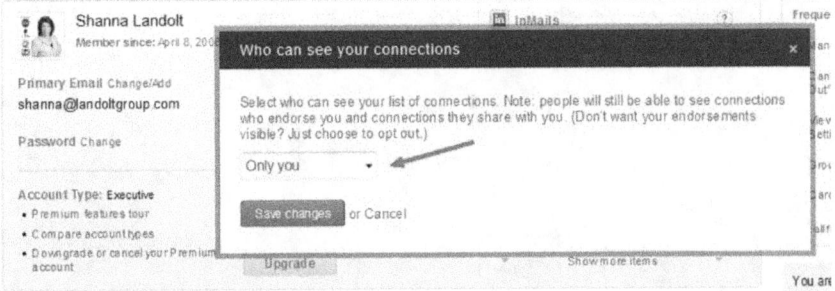

There is a specific reason I'm asking you to do this. I will be having you connect with a number of recruiters and HR contacts who specialize in your industry. Recruiters and HR contacts have huge networks and, in order for you to be on the top of the rankings, these connections are very important. By making this change, this outreach will remain private—your network and current employer will NOT receive a notification of these new connections. This way, no one will wonder why you are reaching out to recruiters and HR pros. They just won't know.

Take Away from Chapter 1

In your Privacy Controls area:

Turn off your activity broadcasts

Change who can see your activity feed to **Only you**.

Change who can see your connections to **Only you**.

Chapter 2
How the LinkedIn Relevance Algorithm Works.

This chapter will give you an understanding of how LinkedIn's Relevance Algorithm[1] works — enough to get you to the top of a LinkedIn search for your specific criteria.

LinkedIn has a system that calculates where you show up on a LinkedIn search. It uses a **variety of factors** to determine if you are on the first page or much further down the results list. And, trust me; you want to be on the first page.

Here are the most important factors:

1. A complete Profile.
2. Be a 1st connection of the person searching you.
3. Have the right keywords in your Profile.

Here is how you get page ranked on a search[2]:

- The first people in a search result will be **1st level connections** with **profiles that are 100% complete** and have the most in-common connections or shared groups with you, ranked in descending order.

- Then it will show **1st level connections** with the **fewest in-common connections or shared groups**. This is ranked in descending order by profile completeness.

- Next are **2nd level connections** ranked in descending order by **profile completeness**.

- Then come **3rd level connections** ranked in descending order by **profile completeness**.

- Then are **Shared Group Members** (outside of your network), ranked in descending order by profile completeness.

- And finally, **everyone outside of your network**, ranked in descending order by **profile completeness.**

You can see that while LinkedIn tells you to only connect with people you know and trust, *their Relevance Algorithm says otherwise*! The more 1st connections the better!

And, if you want to go one step further, connect with people who have 500 connections or more and you will rapidly increase the size of your 2nd and 3rd degree network.

So… What Makes Up a Complete LinkedIn Profile[3]?

A complete LinkedIn Profile must have:

1. Your industry and location
2. An up-to-date current position (with a description)
3. Two past positions
4. Your education
5. Your skills (A minimum of 3 but it's best to have all 50)
6. A Profile Photo
7. At least 50 Connections (But more is better). You can't really expect to be widely found if you have less than 500 connections.
8. To get and keep your 100% complete profile score, LinkedIn requires that you a) update your profile from time-to-time and b) post status updates on a regular basis.

While there are varying grades of "complete", your profile will be truly complete when you have an "All-Star" rating. However, a complete profile without the right keywords will still not have you at the top of the search results.

The 5 Strength Levels are:

5. All-Star

4. Expert

3. Advanced

2. Intermediate

1. Beginner

The Profile Strength rating is found on the right hand side of your Profile Page just below "Who's viewed your profile".

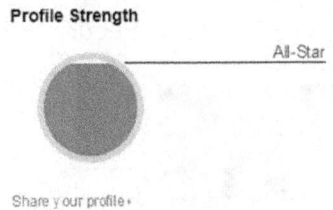

LinkedIn rewards a "complete profile" with higher rankings in their search algorithm at every level of connection: 1st, 2nd and 3rd. The complete profiles with targeted keywords rise to the top every time.

Having a 100% complete profile makes you **40 times** more likely to receive new opportunities through LinkedIn.[4] Google also prefers a 100% complete profile, and will rank you higher in a Google Search.

What Should I Share in a Status Update?

It is very easy to find content to share in a LinkedIn Status Update. Here are a few strategies:

1. You can share an update about an industry event that you

will be attending.

2. You can share someone else's update with your own comment.

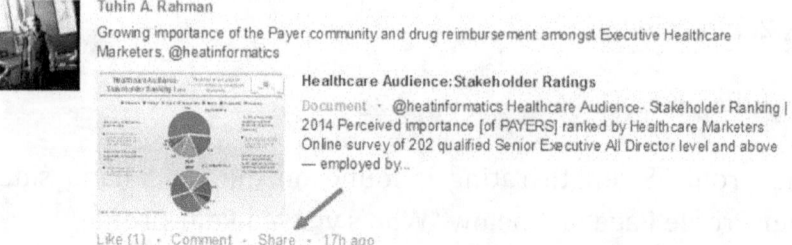

3. Share an article from the LinkedIn Pulse News Feed.

4. Acknowledge someone publicly on LinkedIn for the great work that they did. When you write your status update

use the @ sign before the person's name. It will link to their profile and will show up in their newsfeed as well.

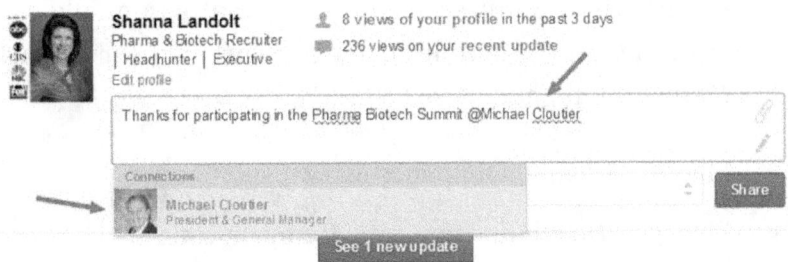

5. Most online articles and blogs have a link to share the article on LinkedIn. When you share the article, post your own thought provoking comment. Or, you can simply mention that it is a great read and why you enjoyed it!

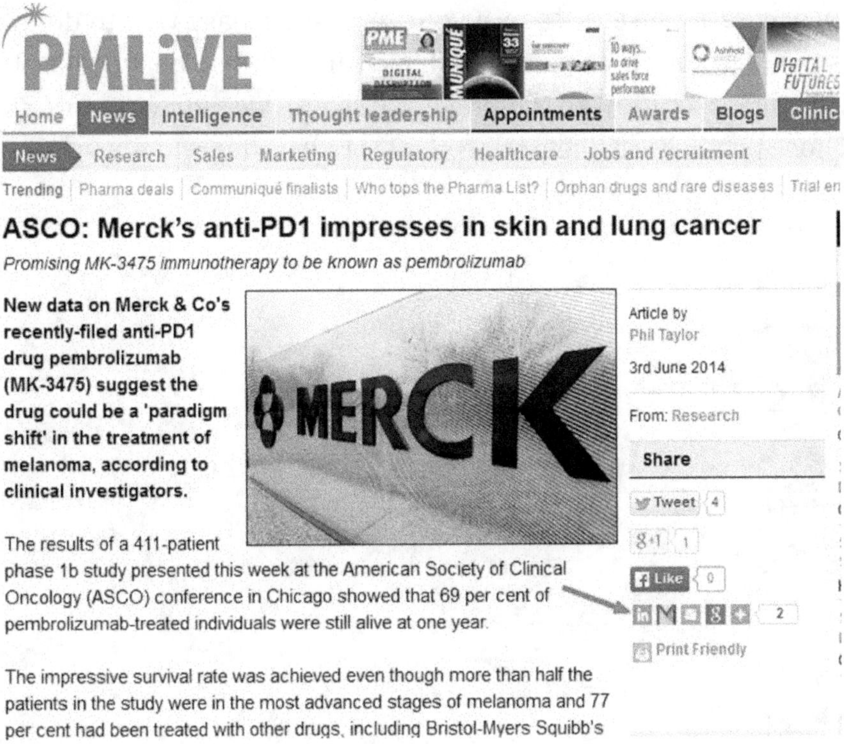

PMLiVE

Home | **News** | Intelligence | Thought leadership | **Appointments** | Awards | Blogs | Clinic

News | Research | Sales | Marketing | Regulatory | Healthcare | Jobs and recruitment

Trending | Pharma deals | Communiqué finalists | Who tops the Pharma List? | Orphan drugs and rare diseases | Trial en

ASCO: Merck's anti-PD1 impresses in skin and lung cancer

Promising MK-3475 immunotherapy to be known as pembrolizumab

New data on Merck & Co's recently-filed anti-PD1 drug pembrolizumab (MK-3475) suggest the drug could be a 'paradigm shift' in the treatment of melanoma, according to clinical investigators.

Article by
Phil Taylor

3rd June 2014

From: Research

Share

Tweet 4

g+1 1

Like 0

M 2

Print Friendly

The results of a 411-patient phase 1b study presented this week at the American Society of Clinical Oncology (ASCO) conference in Chicago showed that 69 per cent of pembrolizumab-treated individuals were still alive at one year.

The impressive survival rate was achieved even though more than half the patients in the study were in the most advanced stages of melanoma and 77 per cent had been treated with other drugs, including Bristol-Myers Squibb's

Now let's talk about Keywords

It's important for you to understand the keywords that a recruiter or HR person will use to find you.

There are a variety of different job titles that essentially mean the same thing. For example, if I was searching for a Market Access Manager I might also search:

- Manager, Health Economics & Access
- Manager, Health Economics & Reimbursement
- Patient Access Manager

Anyone with any of those titles could be right for a Market Access Manager search. Different companies use different titles for what is essentially the same job. Search on LinkedIn for people who are similar to you and see what their job titles are. Incorporate those titles into your profile. An easy way to do this is to enter your own name in a LinkedIn search. Then look at the **People Also Viewed** on the right hand side of your profile. Those profiles are likely to be similar to your own.

People Also Viewed

Health Economics and Reimbursement Strategy Manager

Health Economics and Reimbursement Strategy Manager

Manager, Health Economics and Outcomes Research

Manager, Health Economics and Outcomes Research

Manager - Health Economics, Pricing & Reimbursement Strategies

Market Access and Reimbursement Strategy

So, if you were a Market Access Manager, my recommendation would be to include both your title as well as relevant keywords in your title line, like this:

Market Access Manager │Health Economics │Reimbursement │Patient Access

You have up to 100 characters for your job title: Use them! In the above example, we've used 70 characters.

You could also include a brief tagline after the keywords E.g. My focus is on the Patient!

This example has exactly 100 characters:

Market Access Manager │Health Economics │Reimbursement │Patient Access │ My focus is on the Patient!

A Director of Government Affairs could also have these titles:

- Director, Government Relations & External Affairs
- National Manager, Provincial / State Government & Private Payer Affairs
- Director of Government Affairs & Health Policy

If you were in Government Affairs, my recommendation would be:

Director, Government Affairs │ Government Relations │Health Policy │Private Payers

That string has 82 characters.

If you wanted to include a tagline, this example has 98 characters:

Director, Government Affairs │ Government Relations │Health Policy │Bringing Innovation to Market!

List the Therapeutic Areas You Have Worked In

When you work in pharma or biotechnology, recruiters are often asked to find people with specific therapeutic area experience. Create a list in your Summary section of your therapeutic experience. You can additionally list these therapeutic areas in skills.

If a recruiter is looking for a Product Manager with dermatology experience, they will initially search for "Product Manager, Dermatology". The fact that you work for a dermatology company is irrelevant if the keyword "dermatology" is not in your profile.

Can the Same Thing be Said in Multiple Ways?

- Think about all the different ways of saying the same thing and then use a variety of those words in your profile.
- If there is an abbreviation, use both the abbreviation as well as the full title. (E.g. **MSL** and **Medical Science Liaison**)

The Right Keywords matter most in the following areas of your Profile:

- Name
- Headline
- Summary
- Company Name
- Job Title
- Skills

Now for the Test: Go back and do a search in LinkedIn using the main keywords you have chosen. See where you rank. If you aren't on page 1, go back and rework your keywords! Ask industry colleagues that you trust to search in their LinkedIn account using the same keywords. Ask them which page your profile comes up on. Same deal here: If you aren't on page 1, rework your keywords.

Last but not least, go to Google and search using your keywords and see where you rank. When I work with people on their LinkedIn Profile, my goal is to have them show up on the 1st page of a search for their keywords both in LinkedIn and in Google. Here's an example – they keywords here were "Toronto, Director of Sales, Biotechnology".

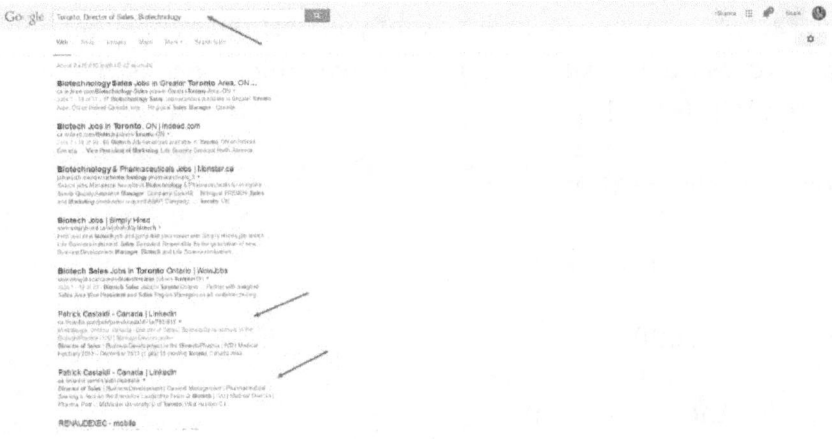

When I optimized Patrick Castaldi's LinkedIn Profile, his was the only LinkedIn Profile to show up on the 1st page of Google for the terms: Toronto, Director of Sales, Biotechnology. Now that's powerful!

Number of characters available:

Since I'm encouraging you to make the most of the space you have to work with, you'll need a list of the Maximum Number of Characters available in each area of your profile. While you don't have to use every single character available, more is definitely better. Here's the list[5]:

Company Name: 100

Professional Headline: 120

Summary: 2,000

Website Anchor Text: 30

Position Title: 100

Position Description: 2,000

Interests: 1,000

Phone Number: 25

Address: 1,000

Skills: 25 Skills and 61 Characters per Skill

LinkedIn Status Update: Up to 700 Characters. (If you want to share with Twitter only the first 140 Characters will be visible.)

Take Away from Chapter 2

1. The more 1st Connections, the better

2. A Complete Profile is one of the most important criteria in LinkedIn's Relevance Algorithm.

3. Have all the elements of a complete LinkedIn Profile.

4. Choose industry appropriate keywords in your profile.

5. The Right Keywords matter most in the following areas.

   Name

   Headline

   Summary

   Company Name

   Job Title

   Skills

Chapter 3
Your Top Box

First impressions matter, so the Top Box is one of the most important areas of your LinkedIn Profile. Many people will choose whether or not to have a closer look based **solely** on the content in that area.

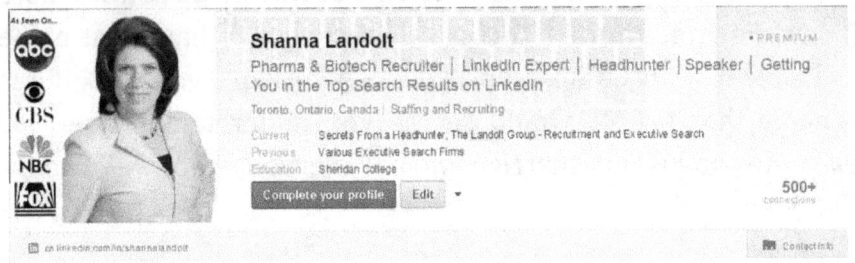

Your Name

This is a LinkedIn keyword search field, so only include your **first** and **last** name. Again, think from the perspective of someone searching you. They are not going to search "Raj Gupta, MBA" they will search "Raj Gupta". You can put your professional accreditation or designation immediately below in the **Headline.**

*Do **NOT** put your e-mail address or phone number in the name field. LinkedIn may penalize you for this and will drop you lower in a search ranking.*

If you have a Former Name, Maiden Name, or Nickname (e.g. you are Samantha but everyone calls you "Sam"), this can be easily included in your Profile. When you are in Edit Profile mode, click the pencil to the left of your first name.

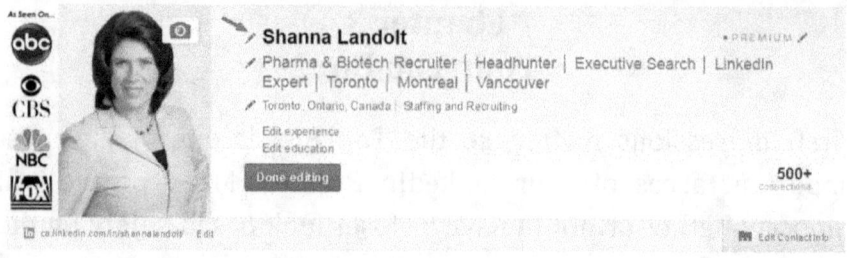

Type the Former Name, Maiden Name or Nickname below where it says **Former Name**. You can then choose to have that name available to your Connections, your Network or Everyone. If it is a name that people would search you under regularly — for example you just got married and not everyone knows — choose Everyone.

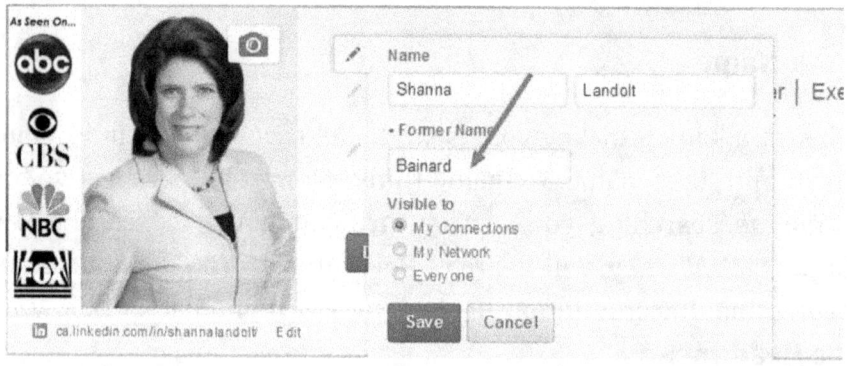

Your Former Name, Maiden Name, or Nickname will now show up in Brackets between your first and last name. Specifically format it this way. Do NOT include both names in your Last Name field. Otherwise it will have a negative impact on your search ranking.

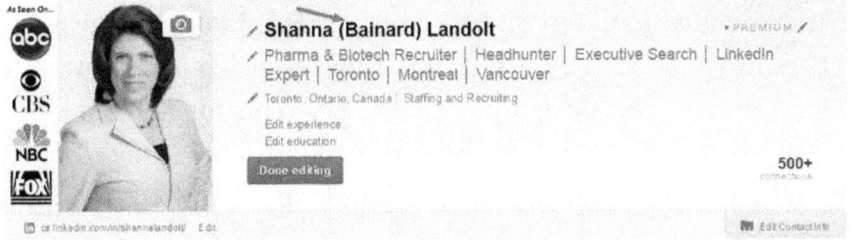

Your Headline

Your Headline is one of the most important areas in LinkedIn's Relevance Algorithm. It will default to your current title, *but do not leave it that way.* Choose the most relevant keywords that describe what you do.

Think about it like this: if someone was searching for someone with MY background, what search terms would they use? Use multiple versions of your title or credentials here. For example, use both Medial Science Liaison and MSL here. On this version of my profile, I use Recruiter, Headhunter, and Executive Search as all 3 of these terms describe what I do.

You have 120 Characters for your Headline. No matter what, do NOT put "Actively Seeking New Opportunities" on your headline. It doesn't work from an SEO perspective or Keyword perspective. I'll show you how to deal with this in the Experience Section.

If you have a Premium Version of LinkedIn, there is a new

feature where you can see example of Headlines or see what others in your industry are using. Don't use this information to influence how you design your headline. The suggestions don't factor in your SEO rating and since most people have poorly thought out headlines this is an example of when NOT to follow the pack!

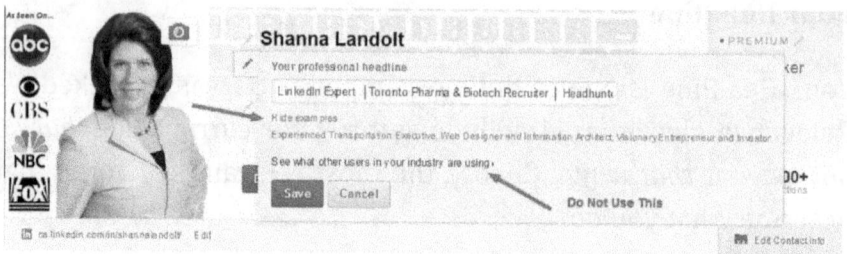

Create a Vanity URL

It's important to create a vanity URL for your Profile. This will help boost your ranking up in a Google Search.

You have 5-30 characters for your vanity URL. You can't include any spaces, dashes, dots or other symbols.

It should be a version of your First and Last Name. You may have to do First Name.Last Name or First Name _Last Name. Otherwise, LinkedIn will default to a version of your name with a list of numbers and letters after it like this:

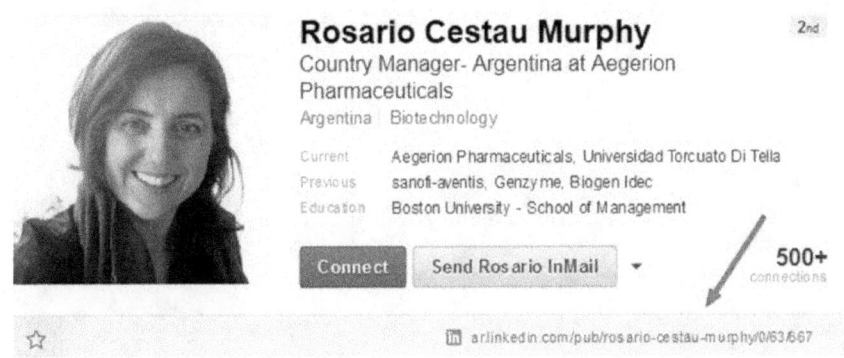

A vanity URL looks great on a resume or business card. It shows that you care about your personal brand.

To boost your SEO (search engine optimization), you can add your top keyword after your name provided you don't go over 30 characters.

E.g. shannalandoltpharmabiotech

You'll notice that I haven't spoken yet about your Profile Photo. I have so much to say about your Profile Photo that I've devoted the entire next chapter to it!

Take Away from Chapter 3

1. Only have your First and Last Name in the name fields.

2. You have 120 Characters for your Headline. Use all the keywords that someone would use to search you.

3. Create a Vanity URL.

Chapter 4
Your Profile Photo

Remember the saying "A picture is worth a thousand words?" That couldn't be truer than with your LinkedIn Profile Photo. Your Profile Photo creates the first impression that people have of you. Make no mistake: They WILL make judgements about how smart or professional you are, based solely on your photo.

Some photos will turn people away. There are people that I have chosen NOT to interview based solely on the photo that they chose. This is a reminder that your choices on LinkedIn are a reflection of your personal brand. Ask yourself, "If I was speaking at an event with 1,000 people at it, is this the photo I would use for the brochure and promotional materials?" Your LinkedIn Profile Photo will be viewed by way more than 1,000 people. Choose wisely.

While you can post a photo that you take with your own camera, if you are an executive, entrepreneur or business owner, I recommend that you have a professional photo taken. If you are active in a job search, this is good advice as well. Actually... I think that everyone should get a professional photo taken! Your choice of photo says a lot about you. And your profile is 11x more likely to be viewed if you have a Profile Photo[1].

Go to the type of photographer that regularly photographs actors or real estate agents. They specialize in "headshots". Tell them that yours is specifically for your LinkedIn Profile and they will size it correctly. The ideal size for the file you will upload is a square, 200x200 to 500x500 pixels, 4MB Maximum. You can upload JPG, GIF or PNG files[2].

The Background for Your Photo:

A white background looks best. If you are not using a professional photographer, have someone take a picture of you with a plain wall behind you. It should be only YOU in the photo – *no one else and no background scenery*. No pictures of you at a party. No children, babies, spouses, colleagues or pets. Save those photos for Facebook!

How to Pose:

Your physical pose is very important. The photo should be shot or cropped so that the area from your mid chest to just below your collar bone is the bottom of the frame. Your face should be looking straight out or your chin should point slightly towards the text of your header line and company. This will draw the viewer towards the text, which is ideal. It's also okay to have your shoulders turned slightly towards the text of your header line. Do not have your face pointing away from the header line text. Your attire should be appropriate for your profession: Dress like you are at a professional meeting. Your hair should be your current colour and style.

Examples of What NOT TO DO in your LinkedIn Profile Photo:

Here are some things to avoid (in a moment I'll show you some REAL PHOTOS from LinkedIn that demonstrate these mistakes)... And, forgive me but I'm going to have a little bit of fun here!

- Head too big
- Grainy or pixelated
- An obvious "selfie"
- Bad lighting

- Inappropriate for your industry

- Party Picture

- Drink or Cigarette in hand

- Wedding Photo

- Swim wear

- Picture with your family / kids / baby / pet or group of people.

- Picture sized wrong

Some real-life examples...

Too Close:

This person's Close Up is WAY TO CLOSE! If you had a meeting with this person, you might not recognize them.

Bad Lighting:

This shot is probably aiming for drama but it doesn't work in the context of a business networking site.

Bad Lighting and... Smoking!

No offense to the smokers, but if you are looking for a new job, do you really want to be discriminated against simply because of the cigarette?

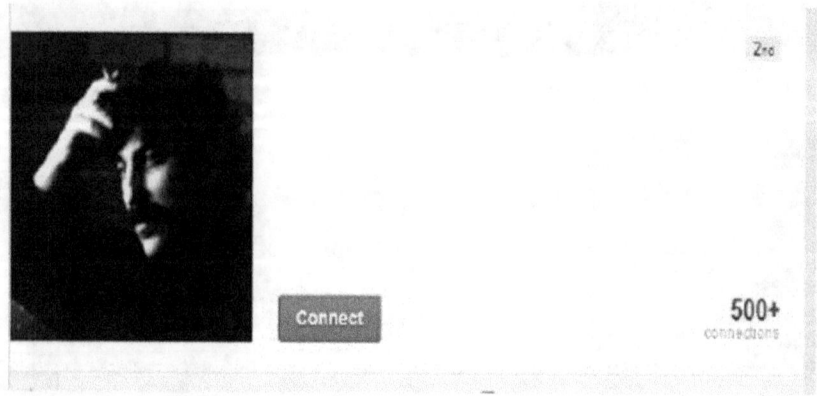

Multiple People in Photo:

The problem with multiple people in a photo is that a viewer won't know which one is you, and causing doubt or confusion is not a plus.

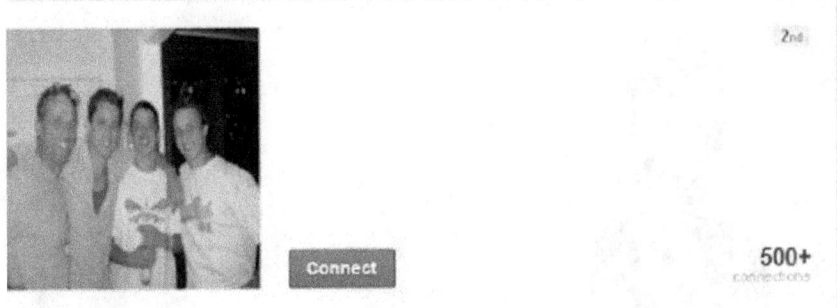

Drinking Photo:

It's just not appropriate to have a drink in hand for your LinkedIn Profile Photo. People will make assumptions that you are a partier (even if you aren't!).

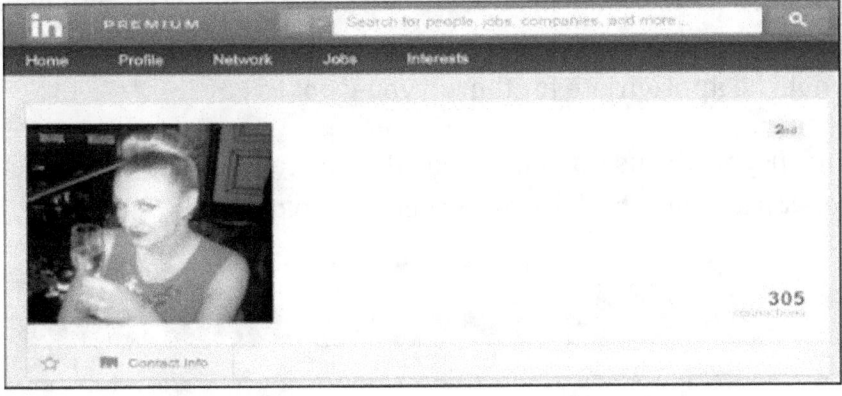

Looking Away from the Text:

When the photo faces the left, it takes your attention away from your headline and the compelling message there.

New Graduate:

If you are a new graduate, congratulations on completing your studies. While this may seem surprising, do NOT put your graduation photo on your LinkedIn Profile. Show a picture that would be appropriate for the job you *want* to have.

And if you do use a photo like this, at least use a purchased version and not the "proof only version," okay?

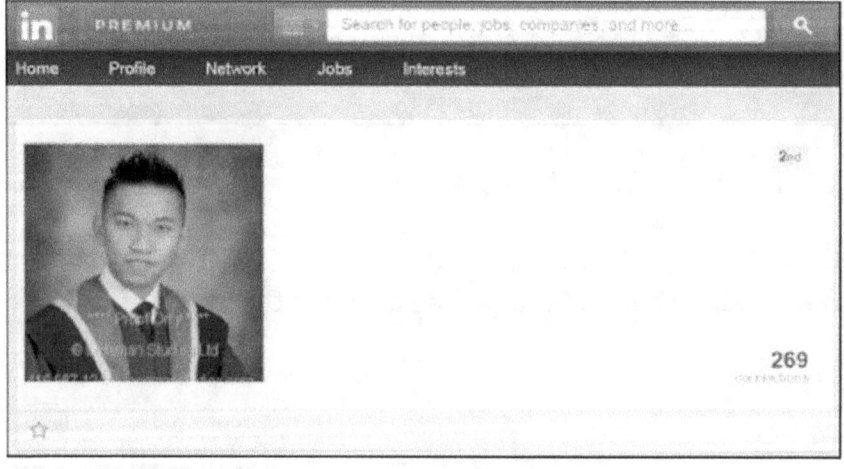

Photo of Baby:

It doesn't matter how cute he or she is. This is the #1 business networking site. Be professional and respect the context. (But you have to admit... she's *really* cute!)

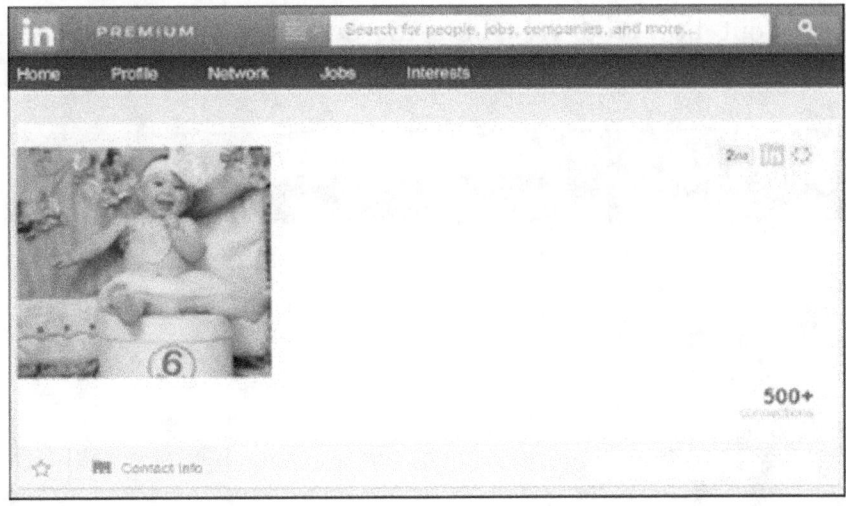

Photo of You with Your Pet:

Unless you are a veterinarian, do not have a photo of you with a pet.

Looking Away From Camera With Child In Hand:

A man and his baby boy looking out to the sea. Maybe it works on a dating site (he's a sensitive single dad!). But just try to figure out how you are going to recognize this person at a networking event.

Wedding Photo:

Regardless of how happy you are or how much you spent on the wedding, do not use a wedding photo. It's just not relevant (Not even a tuxedo picture, if you are male). But... let's wish this couple many years of happiness and health!

Photos at Events:

Hey look! Ran the marathon! Wow... that is a large line of port-a-potties!! Unless you are a professional athlete, a photo of you at a sporting event is out of context. However, you can include details about being a runner on your Interests section. You could even upload the photo elsewhere in your LinkedIn Profile. Just don't use it for the Profile Photo.

Scenery or Object (No Person):

You MUST be the subject of your photo. Do not have a photo of scenery or objects. It actually goes against LinkedIn's Terms of Service. According to LinkedIn: "We provide you with the opportunity to add a photograph to your profile to help others recognize you. Your photo can be removed by LinkedIn if your profile image is not your likeness or a headshot photo. If we remove your photo, you can upload a different photo of yourself to remedy this situation. If we remove your photo 3 times, you will not be able to upload a photo to your profile again."[3]

Face Covered:

Do not cover your face in your LinkedIn photo. What is she doing???

I'm just not sure...

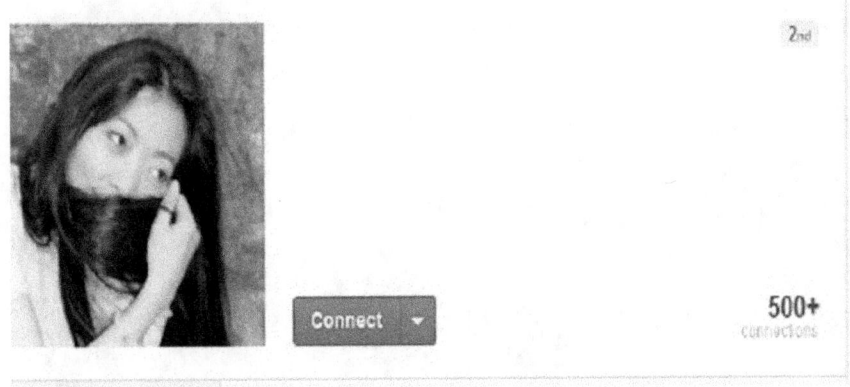

Vacation Photo / Beachwear:

Who needs a professional networking site? Let's all go south and get some R&R!

Photo Sized Incorrectly:

Hmmm - he is the CEO of a communications consultancy... but doesn't know how to size his LinkedIn Photo correctly. Can you see the negative impact the wrong photo can have? He's likely great at communications and just made a poor choice here.

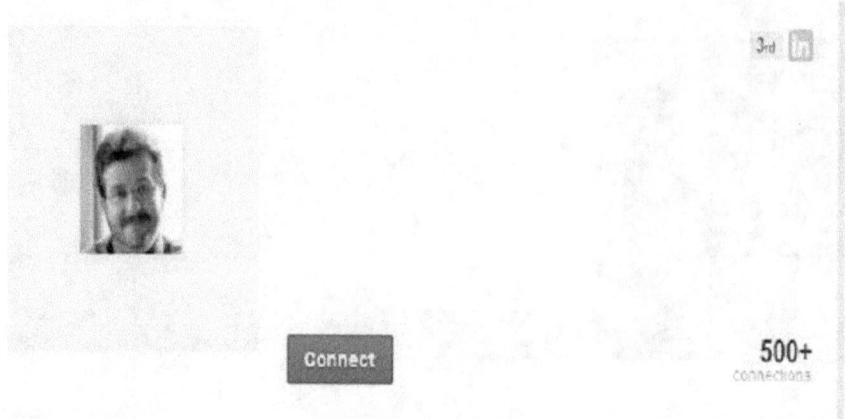

Bad Cropping:

This is just a poorly cropped picture. I wonder who was cut out of that photo?

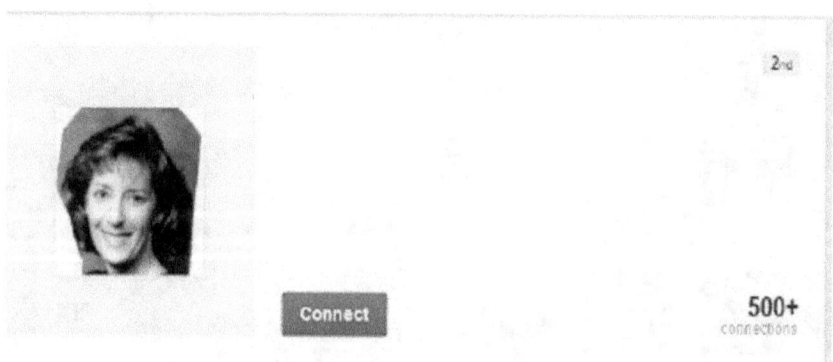

Now, here are some examples of great looking Profile Photos. All of these photos were taken by professional photographers and you can see the difference.

Note how Darryl Vaz's body is facing towards the text. He is dressed professionally. The photo is taken on a white background so there are no distractions. He looks friendly and approachable. From his picture you can imagine that he would be great to partner with.

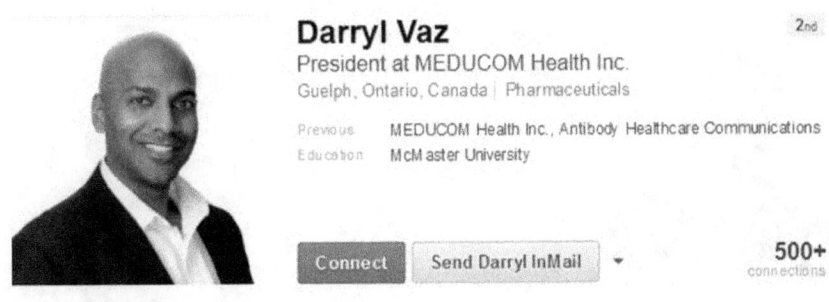

Darryl Vaz   2nd

President at MEDUCOM Health Inc.

Guelph, Ontario, Canada | Pharmaceuticals

Previous   MEDUCOM Health Inc., Antibody Healthcare Communications
Education   McMaster University

Connect   Send Darryl InMail   ▾   **500+**
                                          connections

Polly Israni looks professional, friendly and approachable. The background in her photo is white so the focus is completely on her. She is smiling. The straight on pose communicates a sense of confidence. The picture looks exactly like her if you were to meet in person.[4]

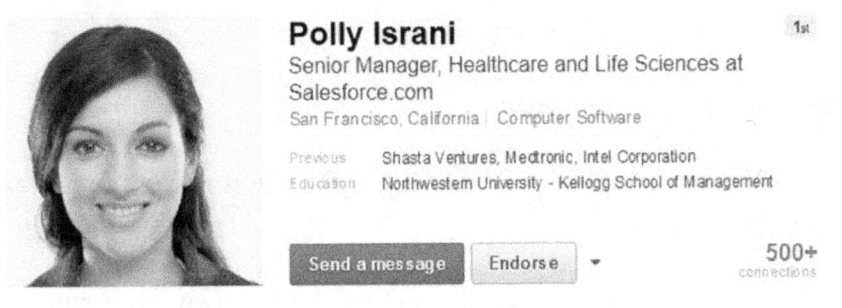

Polly Israni   1st

Senior Manager, Healthcare and Life Sciences at Salesforce.com

San Francisco, California | Computer Software

Previous   Shasta Ventures, Medtronic, Intel Corporation
Education   Northwestern University - Kellogg School of Management

Send a message   Endorse   ▾   **500+**
                                       connections

Jason Lewis's shoulders are slightly turned towards the text and he is looking straight out. He has a confident smile. He looks intelligent and articulate. He's dressed professionally. Again, with the white background there are no distractions. You like him already and can imagine enjoying doing business with him just from his profile photo.

Like I said at the beginning of this chapter, a picture is worth a thousand words and your photo = your online image. Use a picture that you are proud of that creates the right image for you and your industry. The pharmaceutical and biotechnology industry is more conservative than other industries. There are more average and bad photos on LinkedIn than good ones. Take the time to look professional. It will have you stand out.

Take Away from Chapter 4

1. Use a professional photographer who specializes in headshots.

2. Get your photo sized correctly. The ideal size is a square, 200x200 to 500x500 pixels. The file size is 4MB Maximum.

3. You can upload JPG, GIF or PNG files.

4. Dress appropriately for your industry and look professional.

5. Smile.

6. Have your body or chin facing slightly towards the header text.

7. A white background is best.

8. You are the ONLY Person in your LinkedIn Profile Photo.

9. Ask yourself; is this the right photo to be seen by thousands of people in a professional setting?

Chapter 5
Your Contact Information

Your contact information has two parts. Your e-mail, IM, phone, and address are only visible to your 1st level connections. Your Twitter, WeChat, and Websites are visible to everyone on LinkedIn.

You can edit any of the information by being in Edit mode and clicking on Edit Contact Info. When you click on the pencil, it will allow you to edit that particular line.

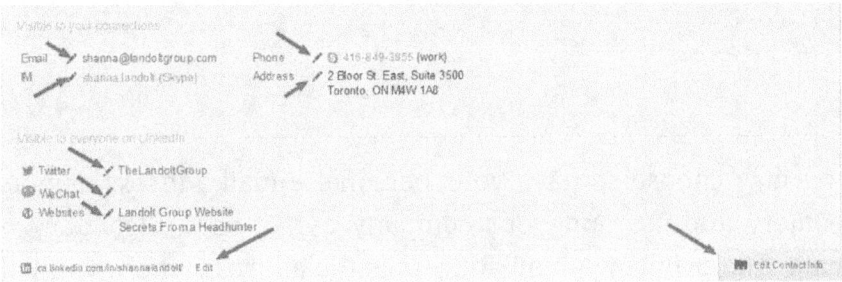

If you are an employee working for a company (as opposed to the owner of the company) it is especially important to have more than one e-mail address. If your company e-mail address is the only address linked to your LinkedIn Profile, you put yourself at risk of not being able to access your LinkedIn Profile if you are terminated and your company e-mail address gets shut down.

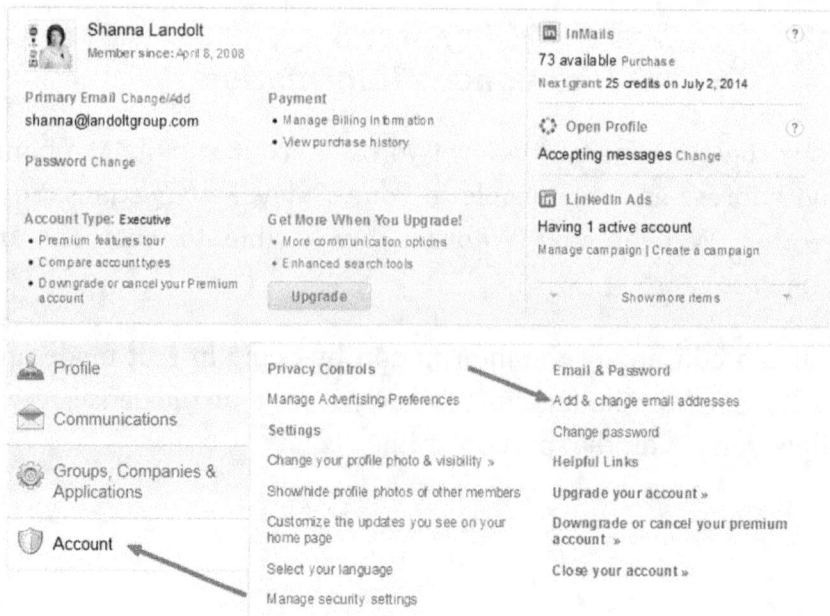

You may choose to have your personal e-mail address as your primary address and your company e-mail as a secondary e-mail. The primary e-mail address is the address where you will receive all of your LinkedIn InMail and notifications, so it's important to use an address that you check regularly. I have three e-mail addresses associated with my account, but shanna@landoltgroup.com is the primary one.

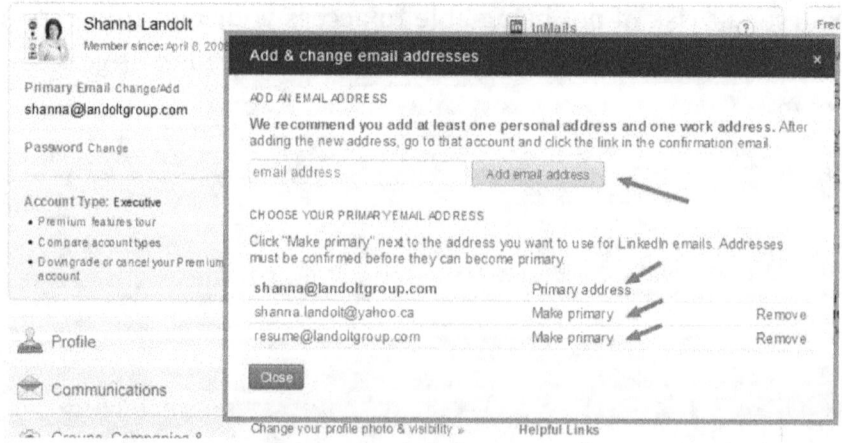

LinkedIn allows you to have one phone number. Unless you are an entrepreneur or business owner, I recommend that you use your cell phone number.

You can put up to three websites in your contact information. I do not recommend including your personal Facebook page. Your company website is an obvious choice. But you can also be creative here. You could create an about.me page or link to some other personal webpage.

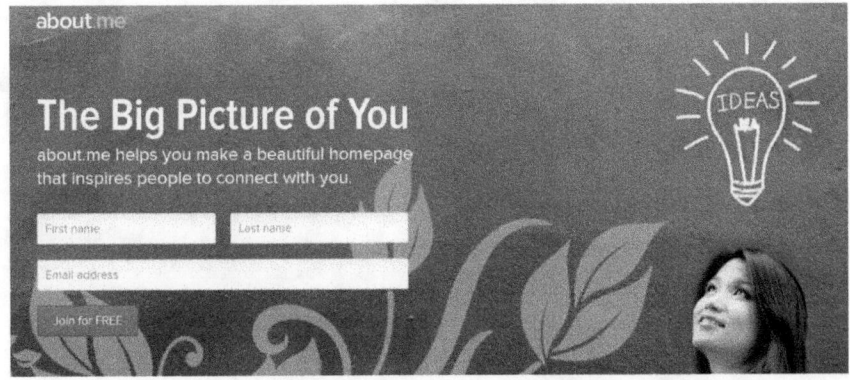

LinkedIn prompts you to use the default terms Company Website, Personal Website, Blog, RSS Feed and Portfolio. Instead, choose **Other**. It will let you customize the website with the name of your choice and then you can include the URL. This will add to your SEO for your personal sites.

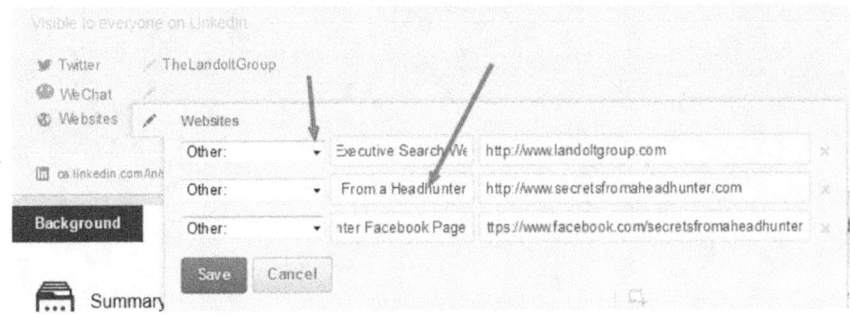

Take Away from Chapter 5

1. Your e-mail, IM, phone and address are only visible to your 1st level connections.

2. Your Twitter, WeChat and Websites are visible to everyone on LinkedIn.

3. Choose "Other" for your website and customize it.

Chapter 6
Your Summary Section

Your LinkedIn Summary Section provides the opportunity for you to say who you are and what you specialize in. It is also an opportunity for your personality to come out. Do NOT write your summary in 3rd person. That is old school and out of date. The social media age is all about personal connection, so your Profile should be written in 1st person.

You have up to 2000 Characters for this section and I want you to get as close to 2000 as you can. Draft your summary in Word and use the word count tool, or paste it into www.wordcounter.net to see how many characters you have used.

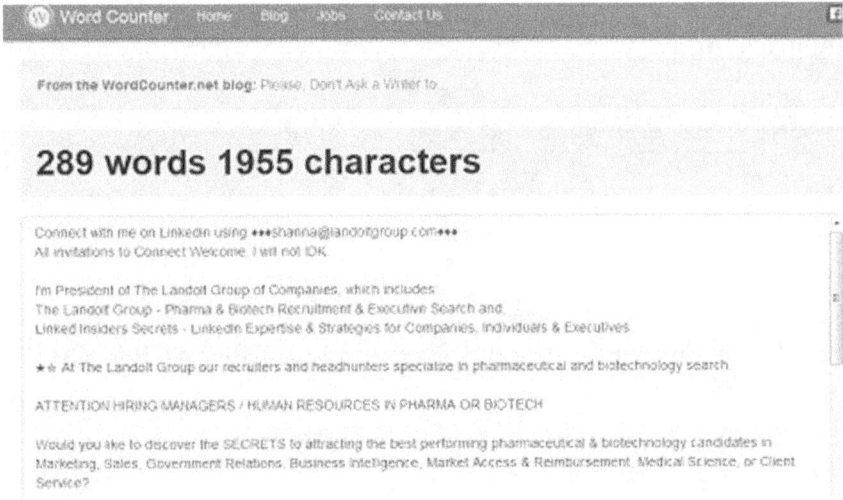

It's important to be keyword rich here. Find different ways to say the same thing, if necessary. The summary section factors heavily into both Google Searches and keyword searches within LinkedIn.

What are the Top 10 Words that a Recruiter or HR Person would use to search for you?

Here are some examples:

Industry:

Pharma

Pharmaceutical

Biotech

Biotechnology

Personalized Medicine

Medical Devices

Generics Industry

Therapeutic Area:

Diabetes

CV

Cardiovascular *Note I have both CV and Cardiovascular on this list

HIV

Oncology

Dermatology

Etc.

You could actually create a list in your summary like this:

Therapeutic Experience: Diabetes, CV, Cardiovascular, HIV, Oncology, Dermatology.

Versions of Your Title:

If you are a Director of Sales you may want to say that you are open to hearing about roles at a Director of Sales, Business Unit Director and VP Sales level.

If you are a GP Sales Representative, you may want to say on your Summary that you welcome conversations about GP Sales Rep, Specialty Sales and Hospital Sales Roles.

If you are actively looking for work, include the titles of roles that you would happily interview for.

Include both acronyms as well as the full spelling of any keywords that use both. Example: HR and Human Resources.

Make sure that you weave the keywords into something that is readable.

List Your Specialties: If you find at the end that you have some keywords that just didn't fit into your message, include them as the last line of your summary as a list of specialties like this:

★☆ At Secrets From a Headhunter we work with Companies to leverage the collective power of their Employee's LinkedIn connections to reduce their recruitment and hiring costs. We also work with Individuals and Executives to create a LinkedIn Profile that is a match for their personality and personal brand.

Learn more about Secrets From a Headhunter: http://www.secretsfromaheadhunter.com

Specialties: Headhunter, Recruiter, Recruiting, Keynote Speaker, LinkedIn Expert, LinkedIn Profile Writer, LinkedIn Media Authority

What's most important here is to ensure that all the relevant keywords are there.

If you aren't sure what the relevant keywords are, check out www.wordle.net

You can cut and paste your resume and some job descriptions and Wordle will create a Word Cloud where the most prominent words will stand out.

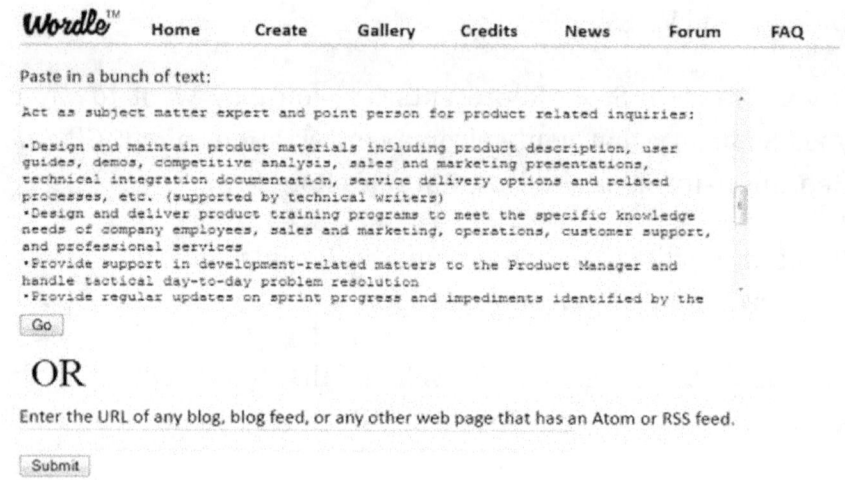

Example of a Word Cloud:

Best Way To Reach You:

Also, include the best way to reach you at the top of your summary.

You may want to include both your e-mail address as well as your cell phone number. The benefit of being contacted about appropriate opportunities far outweighs the risk of receiving a SPAM message. You can always change it back later.

Media and Video:

Both LinkedIn and Google love it when you include links to Media and Video.

If you are actively looking for work, I recommend that you include a 1-2 minute video introduction of yourself. This is essentially your elevator pitch about you. Write it out beforehand and practice it. Film it using your iPhone and have colleagues in the pharma and biotech industry view it. You can also ask pharma and biotech recruiters what they think about your video. You want to ensure that it leaves a great impression. Ask them what message comes across. Load your video up on YouTube. When you publish it, you will get a link. Paste this link into LinkedIn.

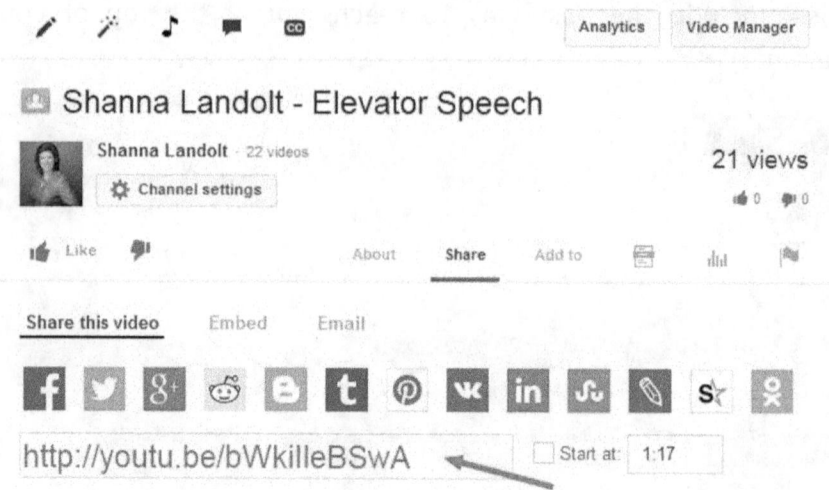

To upload documents, SlideShare presentations, your resume, or a video into your summary go to the box with the + sign beside the edit pencil at the top right of your profile section while you are in Edit mode. Click on the drop down menu. If you are actively looking for work, definitely include your resume. Make sure to title it "Resume_FirstName_LastName" E.g. "Resume_Shanna_Landolt". Don't call the file "My Resume".

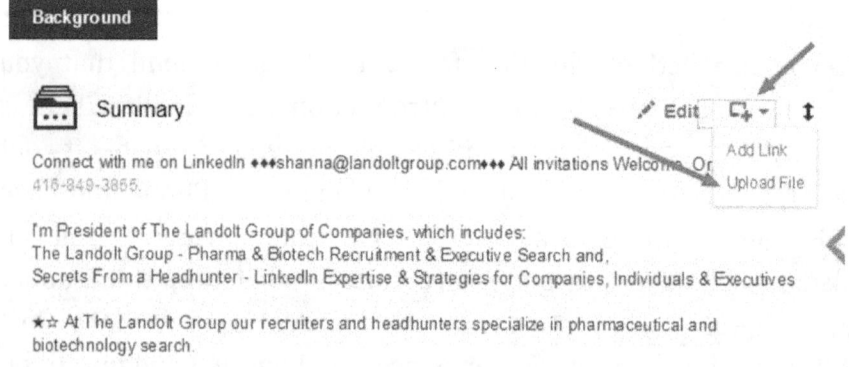

If you are camera shy about videoing yourself, you could include a link to something on YouTube that represents your opinions.

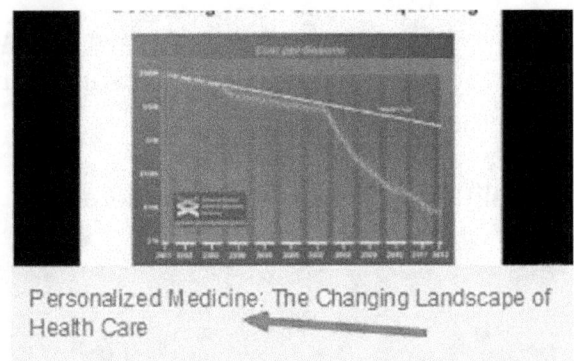

Personalized Medicine: The Changing Landscape of Health Care

Save the video on your own YouTube Channel and create the title of the video as you would like to see it on your profile.

My point here is that having video and added documents really enhances your LinkedIn Profile and increases the odds of you being found. It makes you look current and relevant. It enforces you as a thought leader. And remember, LinkedIn is not just for job searching. People search LinkedIn for all kinds of reasons. I hosted a Pharma Biotech Summit and recruited 14 speakers at the VP and CEO level. My first point of contact for many of these executives was LinkedIn. And, you can bet that most of them read my Profile Summary before calling me back.

Take Away from Chapter 6

For your Summary Section:

1. Use all 2000 characters

2. Be keyword rich and include all relevant keywords

3. Find different ways to communicate the same point

4. Think like a person doing a keyword search

5. Write in 1st person not in 3rd person

6. Don't just have a list of keywords. Use the summary to paint a picture of who you are as a person, your attributes and strengths

7. List specialities or therapeutic areas here

Chapter 7
Your Experience

Your Experience Section is the part of your LinkedIn Profile that reads like the body of your resume.

Here are the number of characters you have to work with:

Company Name: 100 Characters Maximum

Position Title: 100 Characters Maximum

Position Description: 200 Characters Minimum and 2000 Characters Maximum

When it comes to formatting, unfortunately there aren't a lot of options. But you can add symbols for things that you want to stand out such as < | ▮ ► ◄ ♦ • ★ ☆ >.

Here is an example:

Senior Director of Global Sales, ex USA
NANOGEN / SPECTRAL DIAGNOSTICS
2002 – 2007 (5 years) | Toronto, Canada Area

Started at Spectral Diagnostics as the Canadian Point of Care Sales Director and then took on additional responsibility as the Sepsis Business Manager.
After Nanogen acquired the Spectral Diagnostics Assets I was promoted to Senior Director of Global Sales & Systems Integration.
►Contributed 60% of the global sales revenue.
►Developed the Distributor networks in Korea, China, Europe, South America and the Middle East.
►Developed an automated point-of-care reader.

General Manager, Diagnostics Division   SIGMA-ALDRICH
Sigma-Aldrich
1996 – 2002 (6 years) | Toronto, Canada Area

Recipient of the "International Country Manager of the Year Award".
►Responsible to develop and manage the business plan for the Diagnostics division with a team of 9 direct reports.
►Oversaw Regulatory and Compliance / Mandatory Reporting, ISO 13485 Audit process and Product Registration for IVD Products.

One of the things that factors into LinkedIn's Complete Profile

Rating is having a Current Position. So what do you do if you are unemployed? If you are currently on a severance package, you might want to consider keeping that company as your "current" company until the severance package ends. After all, you are still on the payroll. That's completely your choice.

However, if you are unemployed and don't have a current role, create a position called "Seeking a Role" and then say what job you are looking for as your Job Title. E.g. Seeking a Role in Product Management. Then put the industries you want to work in where the "Company Name" would normally be. E.g. Pharmaceutical and Biotechnology Industry.

Then, where you would normally put the job description, you can put a statement about what kind of role you are looking for.

Experience

Seeking a Role on the Executive Leadership Team
Biotech | IVD | Medical Devices | Pharma
January 2014 – Present (5 months)

After successfully positioning Axela's products for strategic partnering and completing my mandate, I am now seeking a Director /VP Sales or Business Development role.

Then complete your experience section. Remember, you have up to 2000 characters for each job description. Put the most detail for jobs that you have had during the last 6 years. Put minimal detail for jobs that happened over 10 years ago.

Sometimes people prefer to say that they are consulting rather than actively looking. This is fine, but you must have more than "Consultant" as your job title or it won't be SEO friendly. Recruiters and HR Managers rarely search the term "Consultant". Say Something Like "Pharmaceutical Market Access Consultant". Again, just put your targeted industries where the company name should be.

If you really are consulting, it is best if you are able to say the names of some of your clients or describe some of the projects you have (or want to) work on.

If a company you worked for is not well known include a brief 2-3 sentence description of what the company does.

In terms of content, put your accomplishments first and your responsibilities after your accomplishments. For accomplishments, think of examples such as:

a. Awards that you won

b. How you made your company money, grew sales or market share, or exceeded targets

c. How you saved your company money or fees or expenses

d. How you saved your company time

e. How you made your company a better place to work

f. Special Projects that you worked on

For your responsibilities include any industry lingo, technical terms and keywords that could be important for your job description. Include both acronyms as well as the fully spelled out words.

Created submissions for OPDP (The Office of Prescription Drug Promotion)

or

Responsible for PAAB (Pharmaceutical Advertising Advisory Board) submissions.

If there is a specific job you are interviewing for, compare your LinkedIn Profile with the job description. Add in any key responsibilities on the job description that you have also been responsible for—using *extremely similar* wording.

If you are really committed to standing out, it is important to avoid sounding like everyone else. Here's a tool that will give you a leg up: Each December, LinkedIn releases the year's Top 10 *most overused buzzwords*[1]. Search for it on Google. Try NOT to use these words too much in your profile.

Here are this year's top 10 most overused buzzwords. How many times do these words show up in your profile?

1. *responsible*
2. *strategic*
3. *creative*
4. *effective*
5. *patient*
6. *expert*
7. *organizational*
8. *driven*
9. *innovative*
10. *analytical*

Recommendations:

Get Recommendations. They really matter. *Research suggests that LinkedIn Profiles with recommendations are three times more likely to get inquiries through LinkedIn searches than those without recommendations.*

It's best to have recommendations from people that you reported to or senior people in the organizations you have worked for. If you are in Client Service or Sales, include recommendations from your clients and customers.

As a recruiter, I will include the recommendations on a candidate's LinkedIn Profile in the candidate briefing document I send to my clients.

It is ok to ask for them personally. You can ask through e-mail or make a phone call. You can also ask for a recommendation directly through LinkedIn but be sure to personalize your request. I suggest including a statement or some bullet points about what you would like to be recommended for and then tell the person you are asking that they are also welcome to use their own words.

To ask through LinkedIn go to the Privacy & Settings Tab under your small photo on the top right hand side of your LinkedIn Profile.

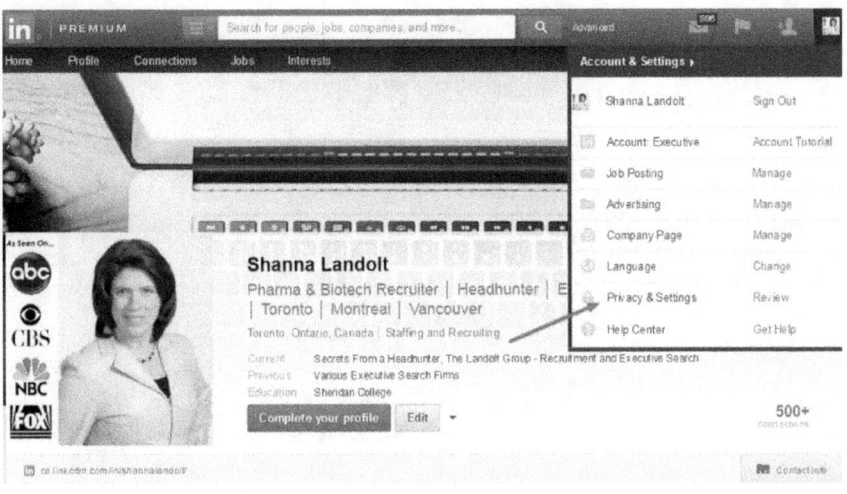

Then click on **Manage your recommendations**:

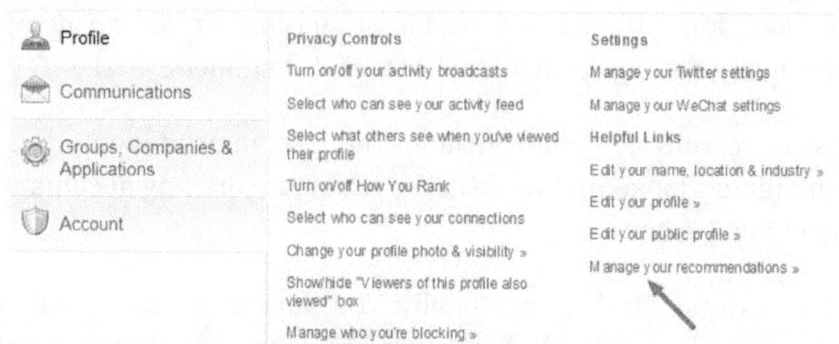

From there you can **Manage Your Recommendations** and **Ask to be Recommended**. LinkedIn will allow you to ask up to 200 people at a time for a recommendation. DON'T do this. Instead, ask one person at a time. The recommendations you receive are date stamped and it's better if they don't all happen at the same time.

It is very important that you customize and personalize LinkedIn's default request message. Here's what it looks like:

Secrets from a Headhunter

Ask your connections to recommend you

1 What do you want to be recommended for?

LinkedIn Expert | President at Secrets From a Headhunter
[Add a job or school]

2 Who do you want to ask?

Your connections:

You can add **200** more recipients

3 Create your message

From: Shanna Landolt
shanna@landoltgroup.com ▾

Subject: Can you recommend me?

I'm sending this to ask you for a brief recommendation of my work that I can include in my LinkedIn profile. If you have any questions, let me know.

Thanks in advance for helping me out.

-Shanna Landolt

Change it to something like this:

3 Create your message

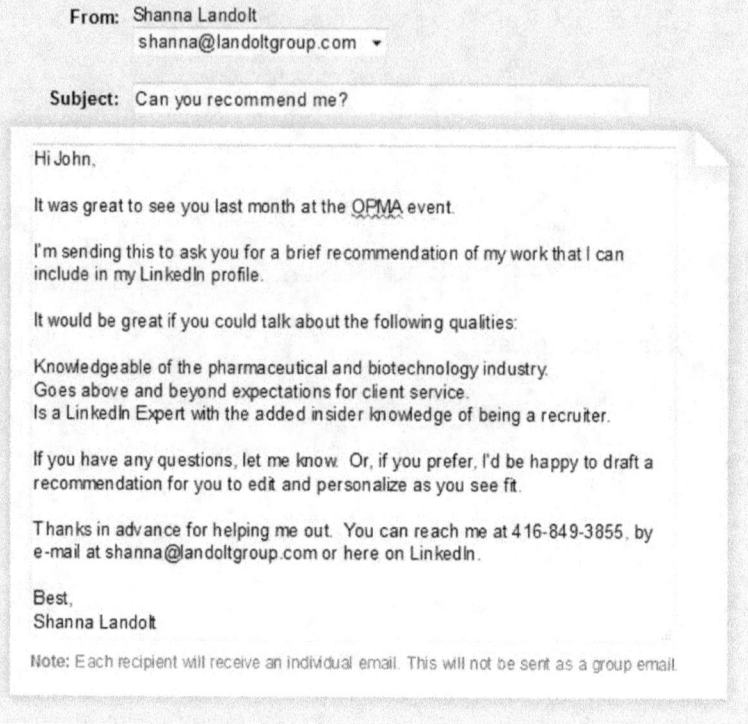

From: Shanna Landolt
shanna@landoltgroup.com ▾

Subject: Can you recommend me?

Hi John,

It was great to see you last month at the OPMA event.

I'm sending this to ask you for a brief recommendation of my work that I can include in my LinkedIn profile.

It would be great if you could talk about the following qualities:

Knowledgeable of the pharmaceutical and biotechnology industry.
Goes above and beyond expectations for client service.
Is a LinkedIn Expert with the added insider knowledge of being a recruiter.

If you have any questions, let me know. Or, if you prefer, I'd be happy to draft a recommendation for you to edit and personalize as you see fit.

Thanks in advance for helping me out. You can reach me at 416-849-3855, by e-mail at shanna@landoltgroup.com or here on LinkedIn.

Best,
Shanna Landolt

Note: Each recipient will receive an individual email. This will not be sent as a group email.

A couple of things to keep in mind about recommendations:

- Don't feel obliged to swap them. It's not expected and it will occur more like "I'll pat your back if you pat mine" instead of an authentic recommendation if you do it too much.

- If someone writes a recommendation and you don't like it, DON'T POST IT. You have full control over whether you post a recommendation or hide it.

One last thing for this section: Just like your summary, I recommend that you add videos, white papers, or SlideShare presentations to any jobs that you have held in the last 6 years. LinkedIn and Google love links.

On NBC Daytime in Tampa

Take Away from Chapter 7

1. Be keyword rich and include all relevant technical terms.

2. If you are unemployed, create a role called "Actively seeking..." and include the industries you are targeting as the company.

3. Put your Accomplishments first and your responsibilities second for each job.

4. Expand more on jobs within the last 6-years, less on jobs over 10 years ago.

5. Get Recommendations.

6. Add video, SlideShare, and Whitepapers to roles from the last 6 years.

Chapter 8
All the Details!

Volunteer Experience & Causes / Projects / Publications / Skills & Endorsements / Education / Test Scores / Languages / Honours & Awards / Courses / Patents / Certification / Additional Info

Okay, deep breath. There are a lot of small details in this section, so if you haven't taken a coffee, tea, or stretch break yet, now is a good time.

Volunteer Experience & Causes:

LinkedIn isn't just for job searches. The Volunteer Experience & Causes section is great for sharing where you care to donate your time, energy, and resources. This is also where someone might look to approach you about being on a Board or Directors, Volunteer Committee, or Project.

Committee Member:

Add any committees that you currently serve on here. You can edit this section by choosing the Edit button, or Add multiple committees by choosing the Add button. This also helps to paint a broader picture of who you are as a person and what matters to you.

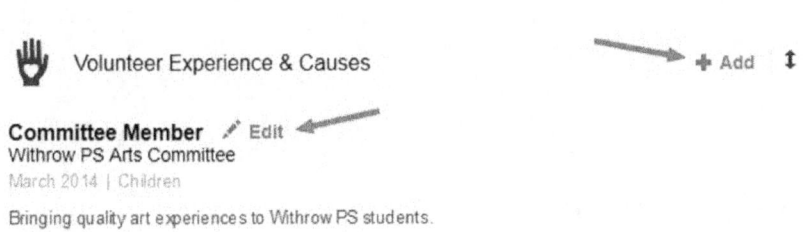

Opportunities You Are Looking for:

This refers specifically to volunteer opportunities. When you click on Edit – it gives you the options to say that you are interested in:

- Joining a non-profit board and/or

- Skills-based volunteering (pro bono consulting)

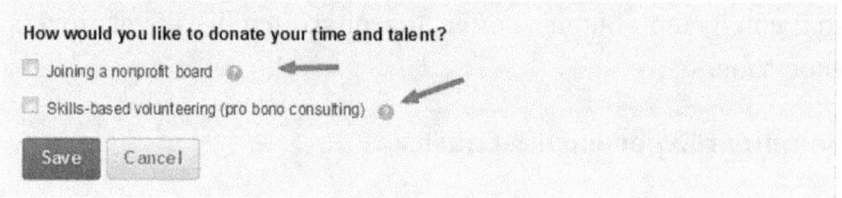

This section is also a searchable field in an Advanced People Search. This allows not-for-profit or volunteer organizations to use LinkedIn to network to find people for their volunteer committees and Boards of Directors.

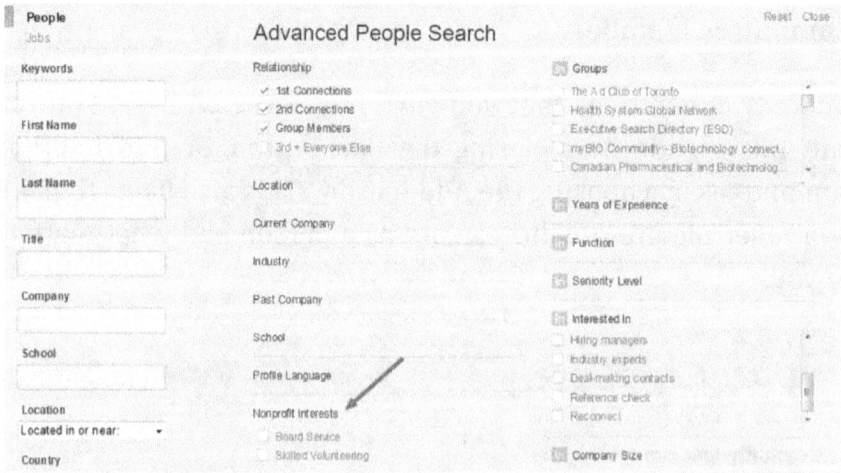

Causes you care about:

When you edit this, it prompts you to a drop down list

What cause(s) do you care about?

- ☐ Animal Welfare
- ☐ Arts and Culture
- ☑ Children
- ☐ Civil Rights and Social Action
- ☐ Disaster and Humanitarian Relief
- ☐ Economic Empowerment
- ☐ Education
- ☐ Environment
- ☐ Health
- ☑ Human Rights
- ☐ Politics
- ☐ Poverty Alleviation
- ☐ Science and Technology
- ☐ Social Services
- ☐ Other

Organizations You Support:

This allows you to indicate the organizations where you volunteer your time or support in principle.

Organizations you support: ✏ Edit
What are your favorite organizations?

- Landmark Education
- World Vision
- Partners for Mental Health

As a recruiter, it tells me a lot about a person and their values when they are willing to give their time and energy to contribute or make a difference. There are also some companies that will actively support their employee's volunteer initiatives, whether it is through financial donations or time off of work to participate as a volunteer.

Projects:

The projects area allows for you to showcase both professional and volunteer projects that you have been involved in. You can link the title of the project to a website, add a summary of the project, and include others on LinkedIn who were members of the team.

If you have worked on a project that you are proud of, include it

— an interviewer may ask you questions about it, giving you an opportunity to further differentiate yourself and speak to an area of authentic passion.

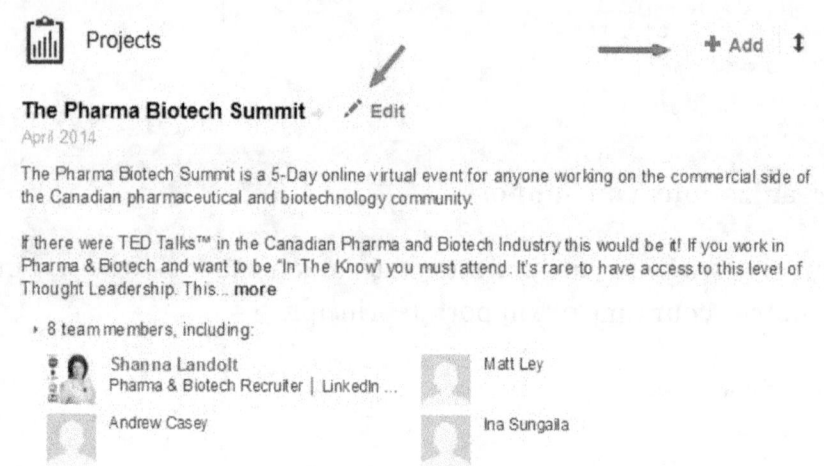

Publications:

If you have been published, include your publication or articles here. You can link the title to a blog, website, or order form for your book. If you have published a scientific paper and there is a reference to it online, include the website.

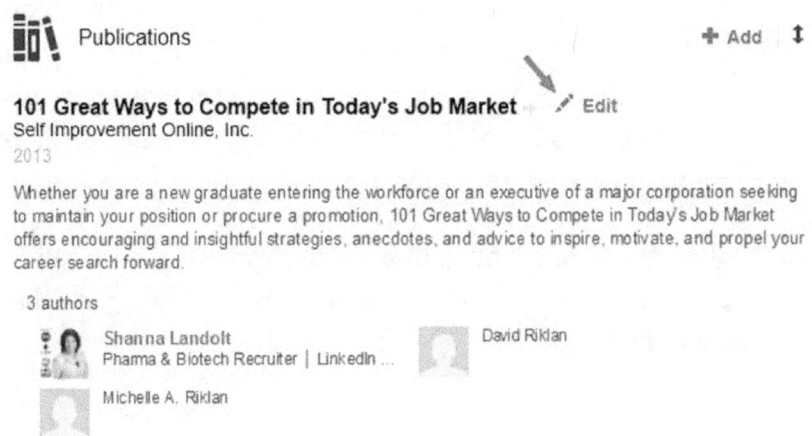

Skills & Endorsements:

You can add up to 50 Skills on your LinkedIn Profile. *Use all 50!*

I know this may seem like a waste of time, but it's actually really important. Most CRM databases that recruiters use will allow them to parse your LinkedIn profile directly into their system. Your skills then become searchable keywords. And if you don't choose 50, then LinkedIn will recommend other skills as suggestions for people when they endorse you, and those skills may not be what you want driving the searches that find you.

The skills with the most endorsements will be at the top. Unfortunately there is no way to make a skill without an endorsement appear higher on the list. After the # of endorsements, skills will be listed according to the date when they were added. If you are entering your skills for the first time, you can drag the skills to put them in the order you want. Put the most important ones first. Trivia Fact: The greatest number of endorsements LinkedIn will show is 99, even if you have more.

It's OK to ask for endorsements for specific skills from people who know you. Endorsements demonstrate "social proof" that you can do what you say you can do. Choose the names of your skills wisely as they also factor into keywords. It's ok to say the same thing in more than one way.

For pharmaceutical and biotechnology professionals, I recommend putting the therapeutic areas that you have experience in here.

Education:

You must include your education as it is one of the elements LinkedIn looks for to determine if a profile is complete. It is a critical piece of the ranking puzzle.

As an added benefit, it allows for Alumni to connect with you easily, extending your network. If you went to a prestigious private school before college or university, add it to your profile.

Never lie about your education. If you are one credit short, don't make it appear as if you are a graduate. If you have not graduated you could put something like Bachelor of Science Program 1985-1988.

Test Scores:

I only recommend including Test Scores if you were in the 90% percentile and above for a test that is extremely relevant to your job.

Languages:

Include any additional languages that you are fluent in. You can choose the level of proficiency. Recruiters and hiring managers will look at language skills with the expectation that you will be able to operate using that language in a business setting, so only include a language if you are actually able to conduct business in it. If you can only stumble through the basics, don't put it on your Profile.

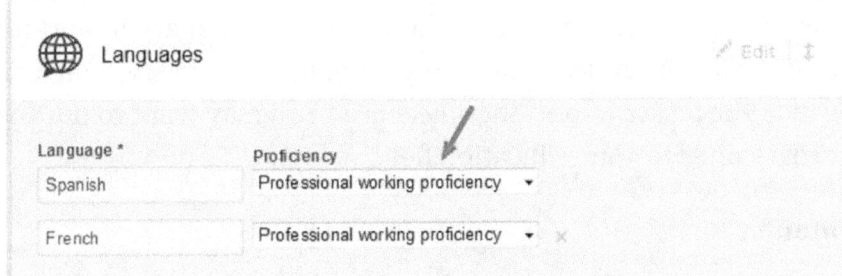

If you work in more than one language, you can create your profile in another language by selecting the dropdown menu to the right of your "Edit Profile" button.

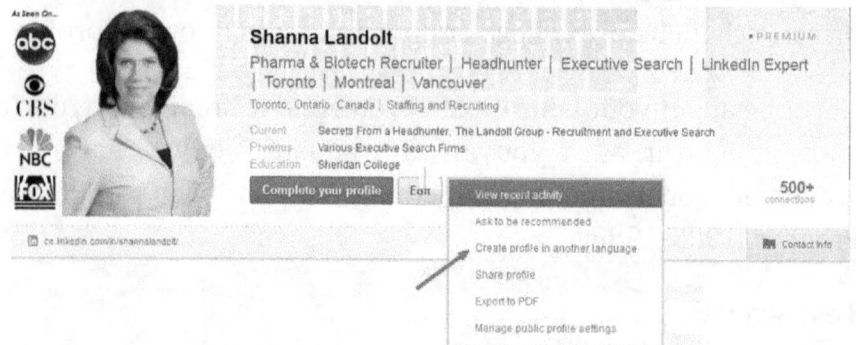

Honors & Awards:

If you have received an Honor or Award, expand upon it here. This is an underutilized area of LinkedIn and will make you look great. Include the date, and include a description of what that honor or award meant and what you did to achieve it.

Note: If you won a number of awards early in your career and it has been a long time since you have been recognized this way, I don't recommend including them. It will leave the viewer wondering "*What have they done lately?*"

Courses:

There are many continuing education courses that are important in the pharmaceutical and biotechnology industry. You can include the lesser important ones here. You may want to put the primary ones in your education field.

Patents:

If you are responsible for a patent, include it here.

Certification:

If you have a certification related to your career, include it here. You could also include an interesting certification that would be a good conversation point in a meeting. Perhaps you took that time to become a certified trainer or coach.

Additional Info:

The Additional Info area includes Interests, Personal Details, and Advice for Contacting.

Additional Info

Interests ✎ Edit

Recruiting Exceptional Talent, Creating a Trusted Adviser Relationship with my Clients, Providing Informed Career Advice, Transformation, Information Marketing, Pharmaceutical Industry, Biotechnology Industry, Recruitment, LinkedIn Expert, LinkedIn Profile Writer, LinkedIn Consultant

Personal Details ✎ Edit

Birthday   February 11
Marital Status   Married

Advice for Contacting Shanna ✎ Edit

Contact me through LinkedIn or e-mail me at shanna@landoltgroup.com or ☏ 416-849-3855

When you create your Interests, put a comma between each one. This will create a hyperlink to others with the same interests both in and outside of your network. Include a combination of work and personal interests.

If you include your birthday, LinkedIn will remind your contacts. It's a great and easy reason to reach out to someone that you have been out of communication with for a while. However, you don't have to include your birth year.

Marital Status is optional. I'm happily married and like to include that. It's a personal choice.

I recommend including your phone number and e-mail address on Advice for Contacting. Some people are worried about SPAM. However, the benefit of being contacted about a new opportunity far outweighs the concern for SPAM. Given it's a network for business professionals, LinkedIn has done a great job of keeping SPAM resulting from profile content to a minimum.

Take Away from Chapter 8

1. Promote that you volunteer or are interested in volunteer work.

2. The Causes you care about and Organizations you support paint of fuller picture of who you are as a person and what is important to you.

3. Showcase both work and volunteer projects that you are proud of.

4. If you have been published, include this as it provides credibility.

5. List 50 Skills! People will endorse you for them. The endorsements provide social proof that you can do what you say you can do, and they are keyword searchable. Include your areas of therapeutic expertise.

6. Include Test Scores only if they are exceptionally high and are relevant to your job, and Languages only if you can conduct business in them.

7. Honors and Awards is an underutilized area of LinkedIn and will make you look great. Include post-graduate courses as well as certifications if relevant.

8. If you have developed a patent, you definitely want to include it on your profile.

9. Include a mix of personal and professional interests. Separate each interest with a comma.

10. Include a phone number and e-mail for people to contact you.

Chapter 9
Groups

One of the fastest and easiest ways to increase your searchability is to increase the number of groups that you are in. You can join up to 50 Groups. Absolutely join all 50. The average LinkedIn member joins 7 groups—joining 50 instantly gives you an advantage as Group membership factors into LinkedIn's Search Relevance Algorithm.

Choose Groups with LARGE NUMBERS of participants. They are more valuable. Choose every group that specializes in pharma and biotech as well as groups that specialize in your area of functional expertise. (E.g. Marketing, Market Access, Government Relations, etc.) Have a combination of both local and national groups. By participating in group discussions you can stay up to date on what's happening in your field, establish yourself as a thought leader, and gain the respect of your industry peers. If you're feeling ambitious, start your own group. It's a great way to be seen as a subject matter expert.

Being a member of a group makes it easy to quickly expand you network. When you identify people of interest, you can send a Connect request and reference that you are both members of the same Group.

Adjust your Group Settings so you don't get overwhelmed with e-mail. Use the Privacy & Settings tab under the small picture of you on the top right hand corner of your profile. Choose Groups, Companies & Applications on the left hand side

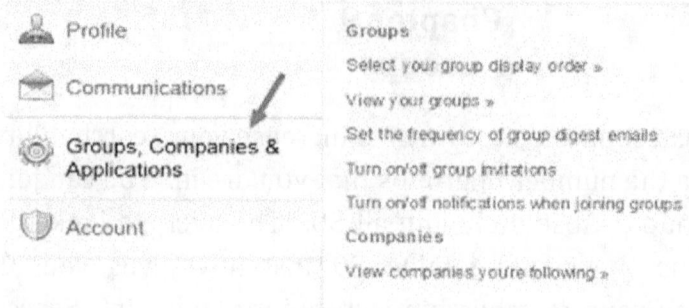

Allow group members to contact you. You can "Follow" group members and will see their status updates. You have control over the frequency that you get messages. I recommend that you choose Allow members of the group to message you. Also Allow the Group Manager to message you.

Display only the groups you want on your profile. Some of you may join groups for recruiters (which is great because they tend to be large) but don't want to advertise that on your profile. That's okay! You can be a member of a group without displaying the logo.

You can personalise the order that your groups display on your LinkedIn Profile.

In Privacy and Settings choose Select your Group Display order. You can then display your groups in any order you choose. Show the most relevant groups first based on your job and industry. You can also change your group Member Settings here.

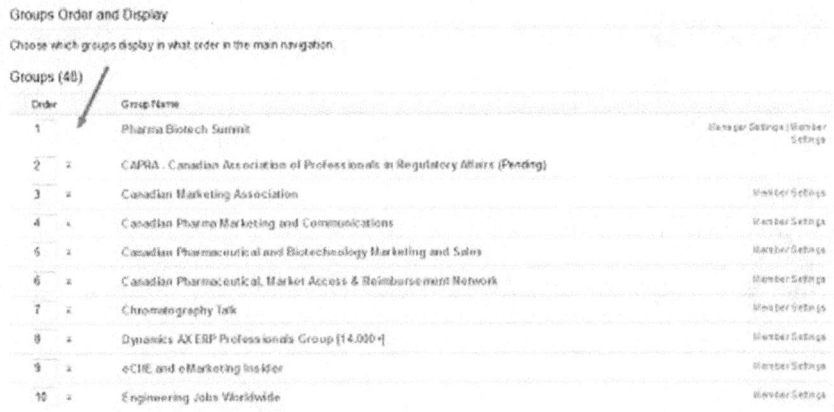

If you want to expand your network very quickly, join an "Open Networker Group". This doesn't mean that you have to accept every invitation you get; if you don't want to accept an invitation just delete it.

You can also Follow Group Members to see their status updates. You can message people in the same group without using an InMail credit if they have chosen that setting.

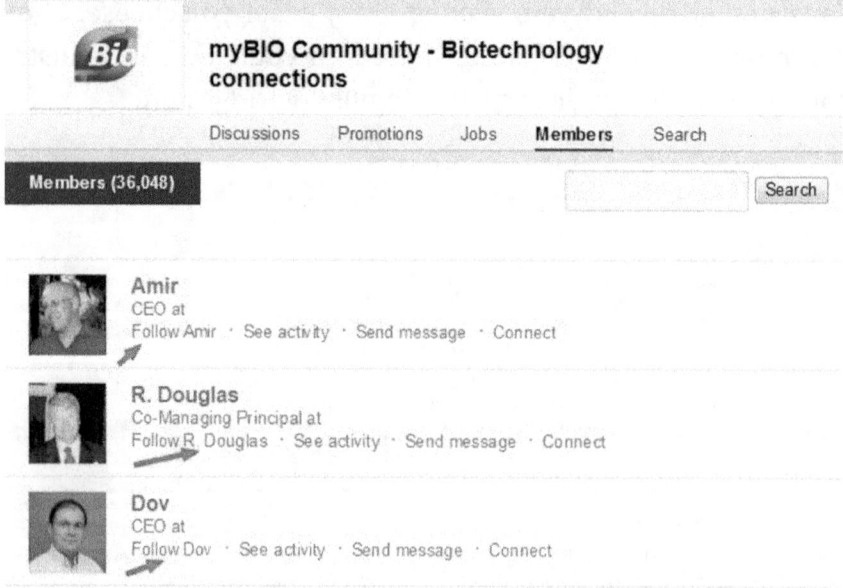

Takeaway from Chapter 9

1. Join 50 Groups. Choose Groups with large numbers of participants.

2. Choose groups where other people in pharma and biotech are members.

3. If you want to quickly expand your network, become a member of an Open Networker Group.

4. Participate in group discussions.

5. Adjust your e-mail settings so you don't get overwhelmed.

6. Allow Group Members to contact you.

7. Customize your group display and order.

Chapter 10
Following Influencers, News, Companies & Schools

These sections are not the biggest influencers of search results, but there is still some value to be mined here, so let's move through them quickly.

Following Influencers:

LinkedIn is great for finding interesting articles that will keep you current and informed about your field. Choose to follow people you are interested in to impact the articles that LinkedIn sends your way via LinkedIn Pulse. A well-curated list also sends a positive message to anyone scanning your profile. When you read something interesting in your feed, forward it to your LinkedIn network via the Share an update area.

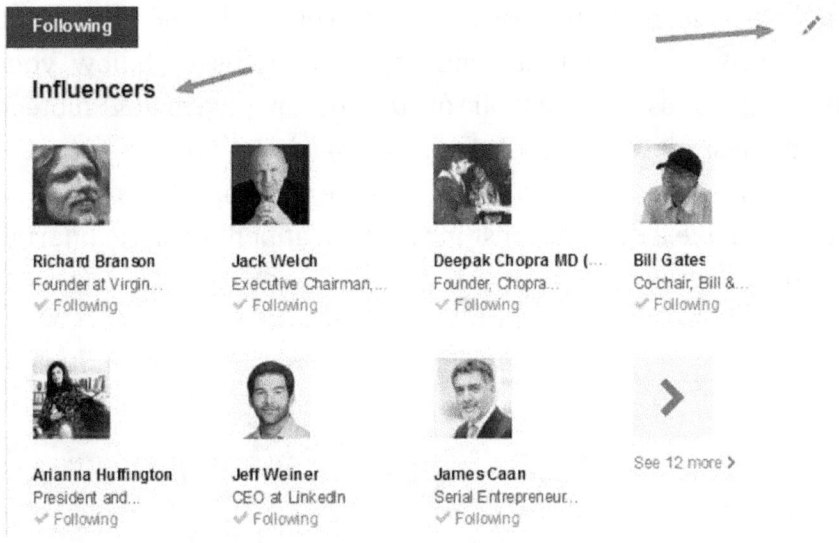

Following News:

Same deal here: Select the kind of news you would like to receive in your LinkedIn Pulse feed. It lets LinkedIn know what you would be interested in hearing about it.

News

Technology
3,252,429 followers
✓ Following

Entrepreneurship & ...
2,909,123 followers
✓ Following

Social Media
2,378,602 followers
✓ Following

Professional Women
2,320,391 followers
✓ Following

Economy
1,947,440 followers
✓ Following

Recruiting & Hiring
1,153,174 followers
✓ Following

Business Travel
694,008 followers
✓ Following

See 2 more >

Companies:

An easy way to stay current about what is happening in the pharmaceutical and biotechnology industry is to follow your competitors as well as all of the other pharma & biotech companies. Stay ahead of your colleagues by knowing what is happening and demonstrate to anyone looking at your Profile that you have a deep interest in what is happening in the pharma & biotech industry.

Companies

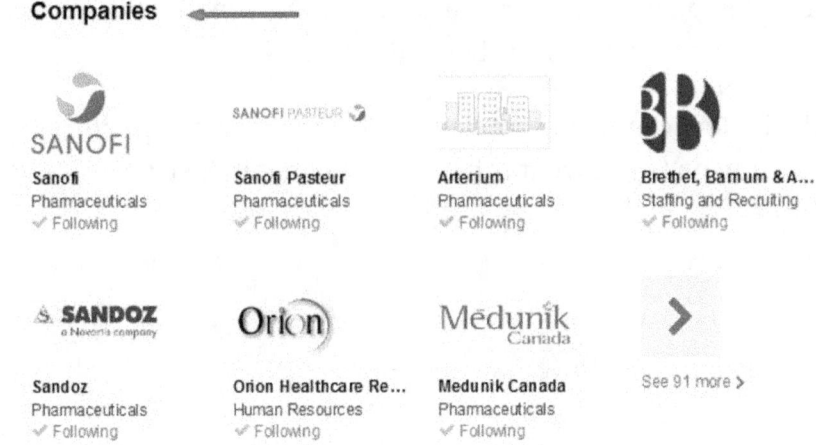

Schools

Follow the schools that you attended to get updates on past graduates; you never know who may turn out to be a useful connection.

If you have done everything I suggested in these first ten chapters you will have a search engine optimized profile that is a great representation of your personal brand. At this stage your profile should be "complete" and you should have an All Star Rating. Congratulations!

The next few chapters will show you how to get extra value from your LinkedIn profile. I'll show you how to conduct a job search and understand how recruiters search LinkedIn profiles. You'll learn how you can become a thought leader by publishing articles on LinkedIn. I'll introduce you to some great apps and technology to complement your LinkedIn experience and give you my thoughts on the Free vs. Premium Accounts.

Take Away from Chapter 10

1. The people and organizations that you follow impact what you see in your LinkedIn Pulse News Feed.

2. Follow companies in your field (including competitors) to stay on top of what is happening in the industry.

Chapter 11
LinkedIn Job Search Strategies for
Pharmaceutical & Biotechnology Professionals

No big revelation here, but LinkedIn is *terrific* for job searching. Given that it's relatively inexpensive to post a job on LinkedIn, Hiring Managers will often post a job before engaging a recruiter, so the opportunities are often fresh and fair game. However, responding to a job posting is not the most effective way to get hired.

I'm going to show you how to search through the open jobs, and give you some advanced strategies for how to handle the application process, so read on.

Click on the Jobs tab at the top of your screen. You can easily search by job title, keywords, or company name. Rest assured that all job search activity on LinkedIn is private. Job views, searches, and applications are never shared with your connections.

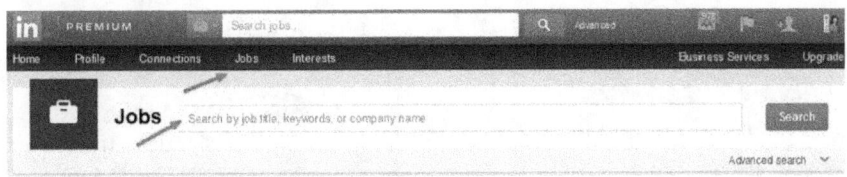

If you have a premium account you can also do an Advanced Search and search by Country, Zip Code (choose the zip code or postal code for the state or province you want to work in), Industry, Functions, and Salary level. If you are unemployed, I recommend purchasing the premium account, at least for the period when you are actively searching. You can cancel and go back to the basic (free!) version once you land your new job. Choose either the Business or Job Seeker version of the premium account. Given LinkedIn frequently updates what is included in their premium accounts you are best to look here to see which version is the best for you: http://help.linkedin.com/app/answers/detail/a_id/71/ft/eng

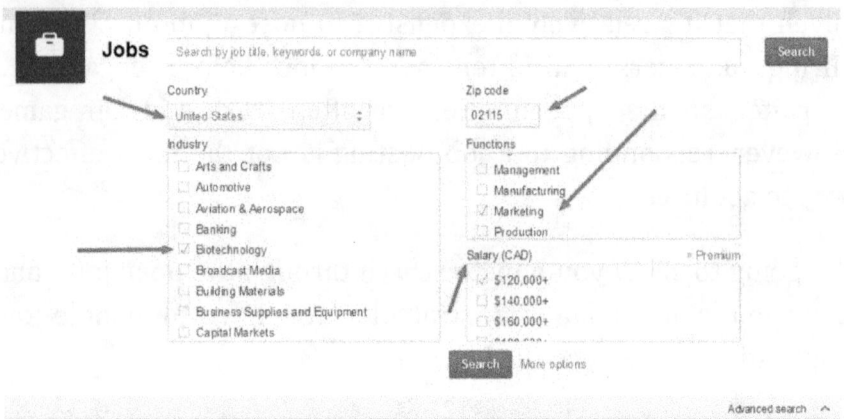

When you save the criteria of a job search in LinkedIn, you will be notified by e-mail when there are new jobs that match the same criteria.

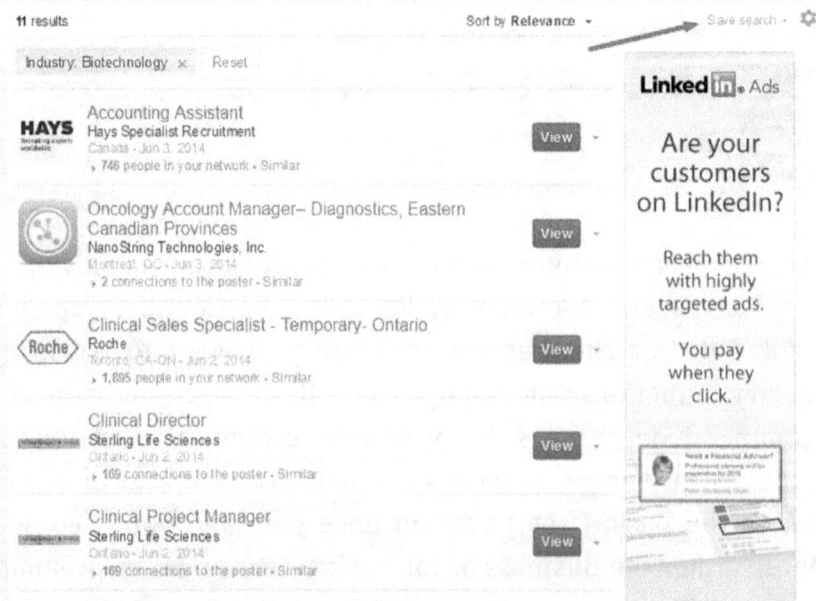

Secrets from a Headhunter

You can choose the frequency of the new job updates that you get and can be alerted, Daily, Weekly, Monthly, or Never.

Tip: You can currently save up to 10 job searches to easily access from the results page. LinkedIn can automatically run your search and email you the new results.

Now, *here is where the insider strategy comes in to play*: DO NOT RESPOND TO THE JOB POST YOU'VE JUST FOUND!!!

The moment you apply online, you become another e-mail in a busy inbox, a number, a statistic. There is no one to go to bat for you and say why you are a good fit. These job postings are cost-saving initiatives for companies and money making initiatives for LinkedIn. When you respond to a job ad like this, you have approximately a 3% chance of being brought in for an interview. Let's repeat that: 3%! Look at the example below. Would you want to be 1 of 124 applicants??? That may be great for the hiring company, but it's not great for you.

Manager, Strategy & Business Analytics

Purdue Pharma Canada - Toronto, Canada Area

Posted 27 days ago

Apply on company website   Save

Other Details

124

Applicants

You wouldn't be in the top 50% of applicants for this job

based on your LinkedIn profile

■ PREMIUM

∨   Get more insights   ∨

About this job

📄 Job description

POSITION: MANAGER, STRATEGY & BUSINESS ANALYTICS

• TWO (2) YEAR CONTRACT

So, what's the secret? 80% of all job placements come through NETWORKING and REFERRALS. Here's where you can use LinkedIn to your advantage to get an interview for a job that is posted without responding to a cattle-call ad.

Do an Advanced People Search on LinkedIn. See who in your network currently works at the organization with the opening. Enter the Name of the Company, Choose Current (meaning people who currently work there), and select your Country.

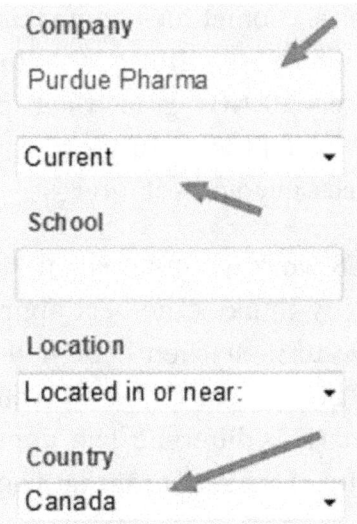

Now review the results. Is there someone in your network who knows you well and would walk your resume over to the hiring manager? Most pharma and biotech companies have employee referral programs. The person who walks your resume over will likely get a hiring bonus if you get the job. That's a win/win for both of you. E-mail or call your connection. See what they know about the role. Tell them why you think you would be a good fit and ask if they would be willing to walk your resume over. Explain why you should be interviewed. That is WAY more powerful than any automated submission.

If you don't know anyone who currently works at the company, do the search again but choose **Past**, rather than current, employees. Is there someone in your network who worked there in the last few years that might still be connected to the hiring manager or HR contact, and would be willing to send your resume over?

If neither of those strategies works, look at the recruiters that you know. Call them and ask if the Company you are interested in is a client of theirs. Sometimes companies will place an ad AND work through a recruiter. However, if the company is not a client of the recruiter DO NOT grant them permission to send your resume over. Even if the recruiter tries to sell you on what a great idea it is, it isn't in your best interest.

If the recruiter DOES work with that client, then strategize with them to see what they think is the best approach. Should they try to introduce you to their client? Should you go in without representation? There is no "one fits all answer" to this question: Each scenario is different. This approach requires that you trust the integrity of the recruiter that you are working with.

Next, without applying online, look at the profiles of everyone in the department that you are applying to and look at the profiles of the HR team. Do not hide your profile and go in as anonymous. *You want them to see that you clicked on their profile.* This is exactly what you want. It's a strategy to encourage them to come after you. Someone might just put 2+2 together and realize that you are a good fit for the role and call you directly.

After that, you could e-mail the person you think is the hiring manager and send them your resume. The name of the hiring manager is usually not on the job description. Usually, it's the HR contact there, and often someone very junior who may not understand why you are qualified. You may have to do a bit of detective work to figure out who the hiring manager is, but it shouldn't be too difficult. The e-mail configuration is usually consistent for everyone at the company. If you can't figure out the person's e-mail address, just call the receptionist. Don't mention that you are looking for a job. Just sound confident and ask for the e-mail address. If they ask why, say that you have to send a message to the person by the end of the day and you don't know where their   e-mail address is.

When you e-mail your resume use a subject line like this:

Resume – Gordon Bekker – Medical Director

Don't just put "My Resume" in the subject line.

In the body of the e-mail say:

Hi _(person's name),

I wanted to take a moment to say hello and introduce myself to you.   I heard through my networking efforts that you are searching for a Medical Director. *(Do NOT refer to the LinkedIn Job Ad.)*

I've attached my resume and here is the link to my LinkedIn Profile: ca.linkedin.com/in/shannalandolt/

I would love to connect with you for a few minutes on the phone. If I'm not the right fit, I may be able to point you to someone in my network that is. You can reach me at 416-849-3855. When does it work for you to talk with me for a few minutes?

Looking forward to hearing from you.

Best,

Your Name

And, if none of this works? Go ahead and apply for the job online as a last resort. The moment you apply online, you are usually making it impossible for a recruiter to represent you at that company for one year (or at least for that specific job), if the company can't fill the role and then brings in a recruiter. This happens more frequently than you might expect, as a lot of companies will post the job first to cast the net wide and then turn to a recruiter when they don't love the results they've generated.

With all the strategies I just mentioned, you also have to use your judgement. Look to see when the role was posted. You don't want your detective work to take a long time. Do which feels right in each situation, but make sure you think through your strategy.

Again... 80% of jobs come through networking, 3% come through advertising. *May the odds be ever in your favor.* ☺

What about Jobs that aren't Advertised?

Most jobs are in what is called the "hidden job market". They aren't advertised at all. This is where LinkedIn is a great - *networking tool*. Reach out to people in your LinkedIn network. Call them or send personalized messages. Let them know that you are looking for a role. Ask if they have heard of anything that might be a good fit for you. Make sure that they have your contact information and tell them that if a recruiter calls them with a role that might be a fit for you, they have your permission to pass on your name and contact information.

Do Not Randomly Send Your Resume to Companies

Do not randomly send your resumes to companies. Especially, do not send your resume to a HR@CompanyName.com type address. You will just end up in a database somewhere. Getting a call from this approach is about on par with winning the lottery.

Premium Jobseeker Badge:

Active job seekers can upgrade to a premium Job Seeker account. You can choose to have this jobseeker briefcase badge on your profile, which indicates that you are actively seeking new opportunities. You will find this in the Privacy & Settings area. (You may have to click **Show more Items** to see it.)

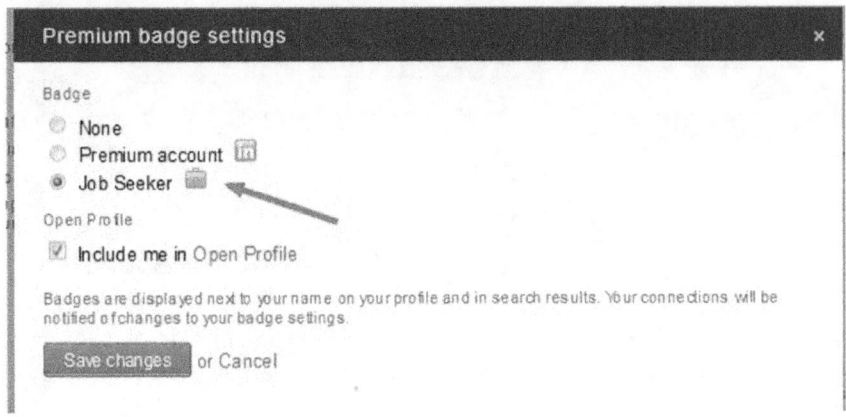

Promote Your Profile Badges:

If you are active in a job search, it looks great to have a profile badge on your e-mail signature. This will encourage people to click through to your LinkedIn Profile. I actually recommend this to everyone, whether you are job searching or not. Go to http://www.linkedin.com/profile/profile-badges where you can cut and paste the code to link to your public profile.

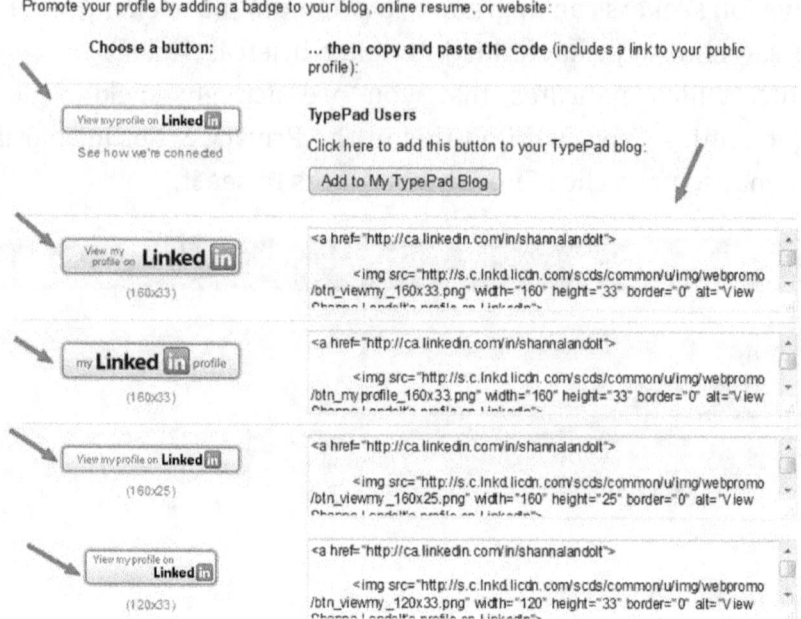

Ultimately, you want to cultivate your LinkedIn network so that people know you, respect you, and recommend you. A friend or colleague is often a more desirable hire than an unknown candidate who interviewed well. Use your LinkedIn network strategically to your advantage.

Take Away from Chapter 11

1. Create and save a job search on LinkedIn to get notified when there are jobs that match your criteria.

2. Review job postings on LinkedIn but use your network to secure an interview.

3. Only get a recruiter to introduce you to a company if the company is a client of that recruiter.

4. Never send your resume randomly to a company. Find a way to network yourself in the door.

Chapter 12
How Do Recruiters Use LinkedIn?

We've covered all the ins and outs of the LinkedIn profile, but there's one more thing that may help you in your networking journey: An insider look at how recruiters use LinkedIn. (After all, this book IS titled Secrets from a Headhunter!) I live and breathe LinkedIn, which gives me the perspective of both a power user and a recruiting professional. Here's what I think you should know....

I spend most of my time in the **Advanced People Search** area. The most common fields I use when I'm conducting a new search for a client are **Keywords, Title, Company** and **Location/Postal Code.** Can you see why we spent so much time on your keywords and title?

I also use the **Industry** dropdown menu and will choose varying combinations of **Biotechnology, Medical Devices, Medical Practice,** and **Pharmaceutical.** Note that the Industry search is linked to your company and what industry your company is in.

So, if I was searching for a Product Manager with Diabetes experience, I would put "Diabetes" in the Keywords section. Then I would put "Product Manager" in the Title area and choose the "Current" title option. Then I would put in a postal code that is close to the company and choose people who live within 50 mi (80 km)

I can then save that search and set an Alert for LinkedIn to notify me every time there is a new person who matches my search criteria.

Saved Searches

Type	Title	New	Alert	Created			
People	Diabetes Product Manager		Daily		⇕	✓	⊗
People	Montreal Pharma Biotech Summit	16	Weekly	Feb 28, 2014	✎	✗	

Next I would do a broader search and would look at all the Product Managers in pharma and biotech who fit the right geographic area.

Then I would look at people who were Product Managers in the past.

Finally, I would search by expanding the geographic area to include people who might have to relocate.

Remember, the LinkedIn Relevance Algorithm will show me the people who match all of my keyword, industry, and location criteria in the following order[1]:

- The first people in a search result will be my **1st level connections** with **profiles that are 100% complete** and have the most in-common connections or shared groups with me. This is ranked in descending order.

- Then it will show my **1st level connections** with the **fewest in-common connections or shared groups**. This is ranked in descending order by profile completeness.

- Next I will see **2nd level connections** ranked in descending order by **profile completeness**.

- Then I will see **3rd level connections** ranked in descending order by **profile completeness**.

- Then I will see **Shared Group Members** (outside of my network), ranked in descending order by profile completeness.

- And finally, **everyone outside of my network**, ranked in descending order by **profile completeness**.

Often people are worried about connecting with recruiters because they are not actively looking for work or don't want their other connections or employers to know. Ultimately, I believe it's in *your* best interest to connect with all the recruiters who specialize in pharma and biotech. If you are in a recruiter's network and have appropriately keyword optimized your LinkedIn Profile, then you will always be in the first search results for roles that are a fit for your background, skills, and LinkedIn Profile. I will also receive a notification if you change jobs, if we're connected.

To reduce any discomfort you may have connecting with recruiters, make sure that you have adjusted your privacy settings like we discussed in Chapter 1, so you don't notify everyone that you are connecting with recruiters. When reaching out, you could also send a note like this:

"Hi, I wanted to reach out to you because I work in the pharmaceutical and biotechnology industry and know you specialize in this area. While I'm not actively looking for work, I always appreciate being contacted about roles that are appropriate for my experience and would appreciate being in your network. You are welcome to reach out to me if there is every anyway I can help you in the future."

It's in *your* best interest to connect with all the recruiters who specialize in pharma and biotech. Most of them will have larger networks than you do, so you win by being affiliated with them.

Just make sure that you have adjusted your privacy settings like we discussed earlier so you don't notify everyone that you are connecting with recruiters:

Step #1: In the same **Privacy and Settings** area choose **Select who can see your activity feed**.

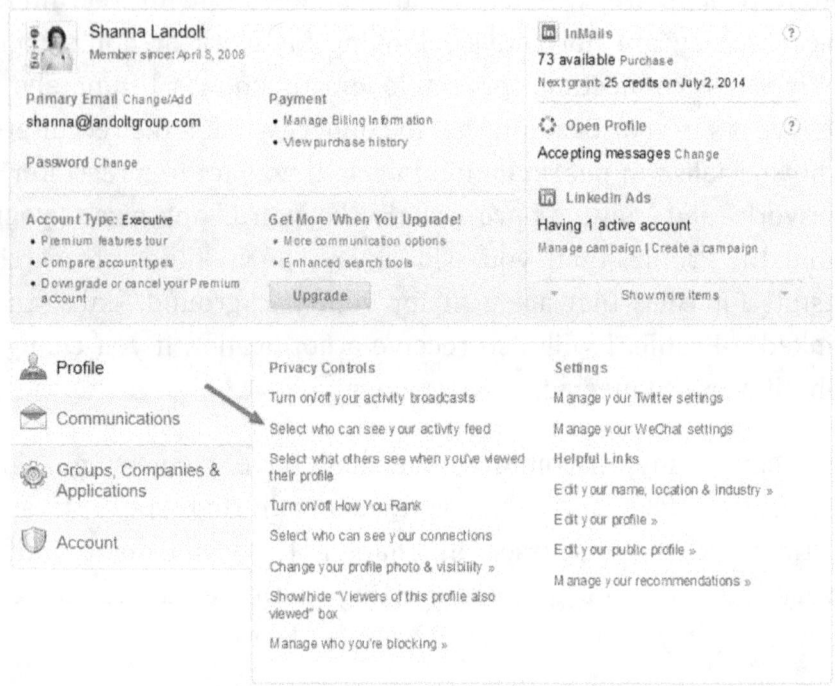

Step #2: Choose **Only you** on the drop down menu and save changes.

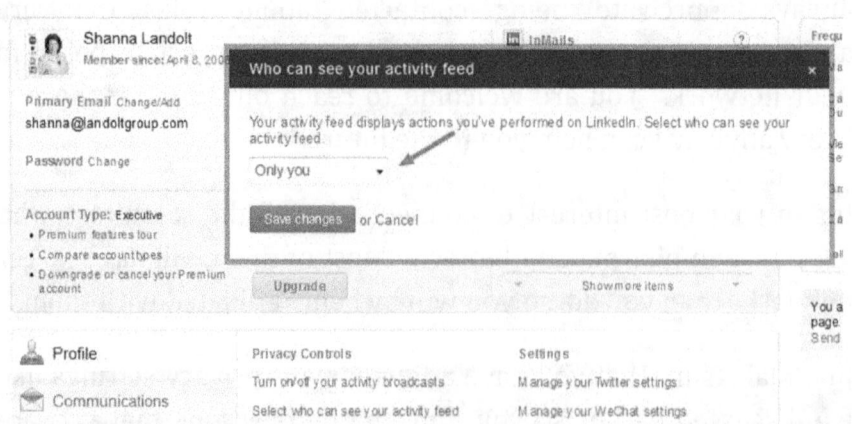

Now you won't be notifying everyone in your network each time you make a new connection.

Step #3: Select **Who can see your connections**.

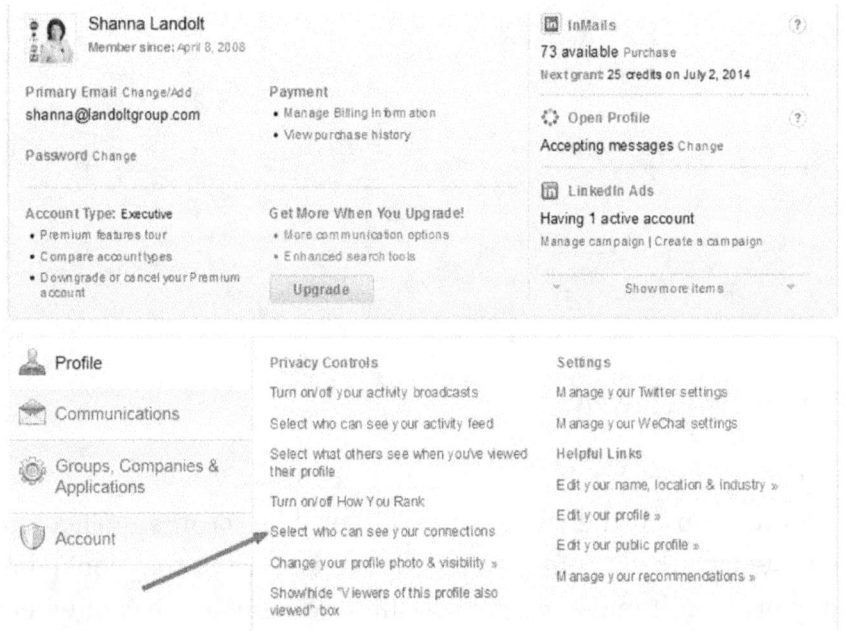

Step #4: Select **Only You** on the drop down menu and then save changes. This will prevent people from combing through your network to see who you are connected with.

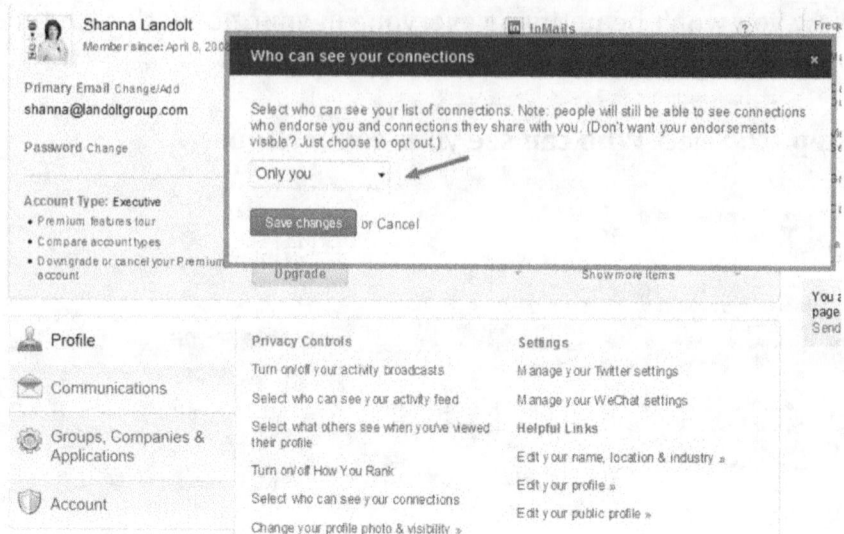

People Also Viewed:

Recruiters will also look at the **People Also Viewed** area that will show up on the right hand side of your profile. This will show what other profiles people looked at when they looked at your profile. It may give the recruiter some new ideas of where to look for leads and combines the intelligence of other LinkedIn Profile viewers.

People Also Viewed

 Head of Human Resources/Head of Compliance at

 VP HR at

 Vice President, Human Resources at

 HR Generalist at

 Head of Human Resources Toronto at

 Vice President, Human Resources at

 Vice President Sales and Marketing at

As a recruiter I pay extra special attention to **Recommendations.** If I'm interviewing a candidate, I read those Recommendations. I also will include them in a briefing report that I send to my clients. It's like a mini-reference check. In the pharmaceutical and biotechnology industry, people operate at such a high standard of integrity that they won't usually post something publicly like this if they don't really mean it. Simply put, if a candidate has Recommendations on their LinkedIn profile and the other candidates don't, the one with Recommendations has a competitive advantage.

I also use TAGS in LinkedIn. If you are connected to me and work in the pharmaceutical or biotechnology industry, I will TAG you in my Contacts according to your expertise. Then when I'm doing a search for someone with your expertise, I can easily identify you and send you a message asking if you are interested in learning more about the role that I'm am recruiting for.

Filter by **All Contacts** ▾

‹ Tag

1 pharma sales rep

1 pharma sales trainer

1 pharma spec sales

1 pharma vp dir
business development

1 pharma vp dir medical
affairs

1 pharma vp dir public
affairs

1 pharma vp sales

1 pharma vp sales &
marketing

1 pharma vp/dir market
access

Setting up TAGS is also a great way for you to organize your contacts. Don't feel that you have to tag everyone, just people you would want to reach easily by category. For example, you might TAG everyone in HR, or all recruiters, so you can easily send them all a message if you were initiating a job search.

When I'm doing a search I will include a status update about the roles that I'm recruiting for. I will also network with people who are either too junior or too senior who may know someone appropriate. If I don't have contact information to call or e-mail them, I will send them a LinkedIn InMail.

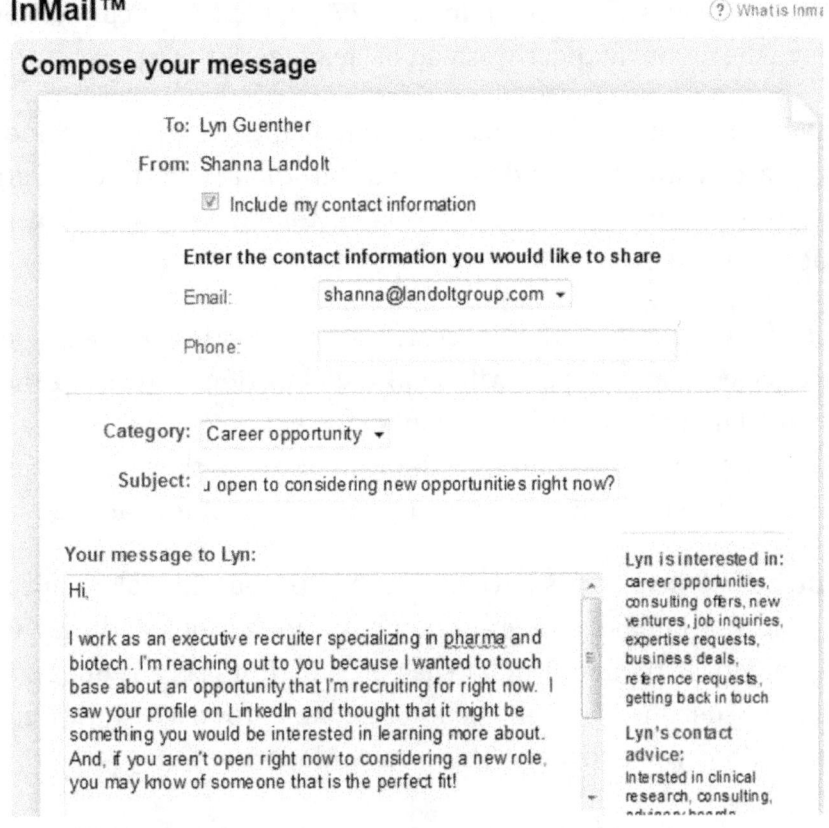

My CRM Database connects with LinkedIn and I can choose to pull in or parse a LinkedIn Profile that is the right fit for a search (whether we are first connections or not). If we **are** first connections, my database will also pull all of your contact information from LinkedIn into my system.

Recruiters will also look at the content of your LinkedIn Profile. And yes, we're judgmental! Like it or not, it will make you look more progressive if your profile is great. You could be labelled "old school" if you just have a minimal profile.

Spelling errors stand out and make you look sloppy. Just for fun I did an Advanced Search and put "manger" in the title field and "pharmaceutical" as the industry. 77 people in my connections have the error "manger" instead of "manager".

And your photo... let's just say that I've decided not to move forward with a candidate based on their choice of profile photo—I view it as an indication of their professionalism (or lack thereof).

Have you noticed that recruiters are starting to send you messages asking if you will send a connection request to them instead of just sending you a LinkedIn request? That is because LinkedIn has a maximum of 3000 invitations that can be sent. The recruiters are likely saving up their stock of invitations!

After 3000 invitations have been used up, you can make a special request of LinkedIn to grant you more invitations and they will usually pass them out in batches of 100. But it is a request, and can be declined. You used to be able to track how many invitations you had sent. This is now hidden.

TheLadders.com is a comprehensive job-matching service and employment website for career-driven professionals. They released a study in 2014 to track recruiter behaviour. They used eye tracking-based "heat maps" to track recruiters eye movements when they looked at LinkedIn profiles. It showed that recruiters fixated for an average of 19% of the total time on profile pictures.   I can't stress enough the importance of a professional Profile Photo.

Here is a heat map that demonstrates recruiter eye-movement on LinkedIn Profiles:

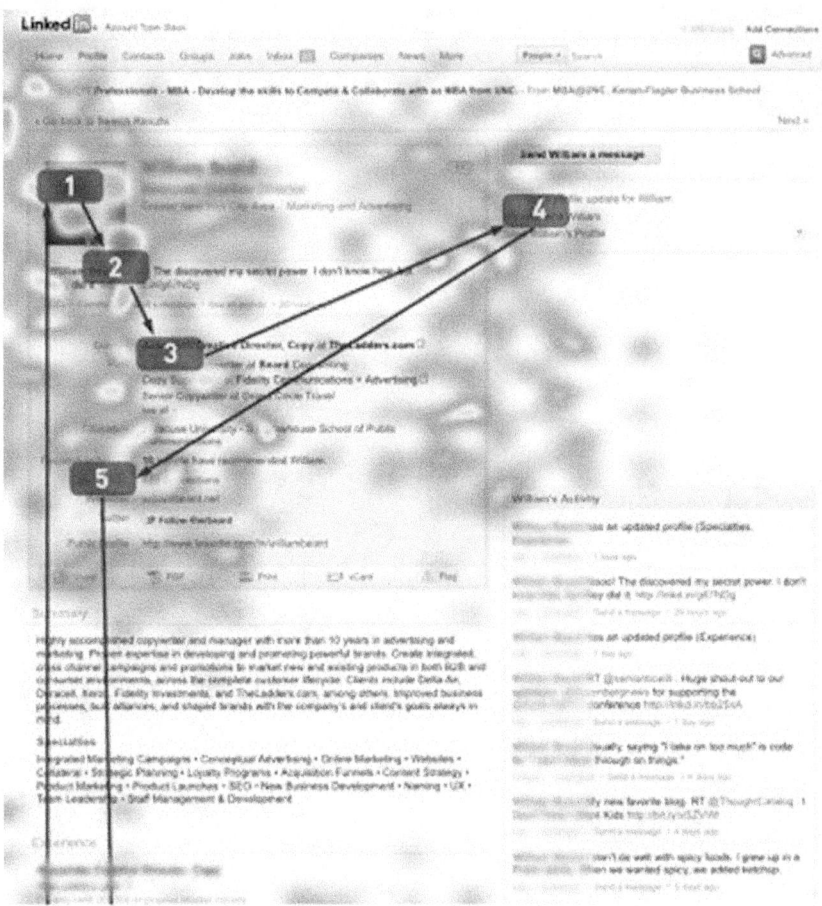

Chapter 13
Publish on LinkedIn

In 2014, LinkedIn created a publishing platform that enables you to write an article, publish it on LinkedIn and distribute it to your connections. If enough people read / share / like it, LinkedIn's publishing platform will give it wider distribution. The benefits of this should be obvious! Writing about what's happening in a therapeutic area or about trends in pharma or biotech is a great way to expand your network and be recognized as a thought leader.

The publishing platform is in the process of being rolled out as I write this, so the first step is to check whether it has been enabled on your platform yet. When you sign in to LinkedIn, look for a pencil on the right hand side of your Share an update bar. If you see it, you have access to the platform — if not, don't worry, it's coming soon!

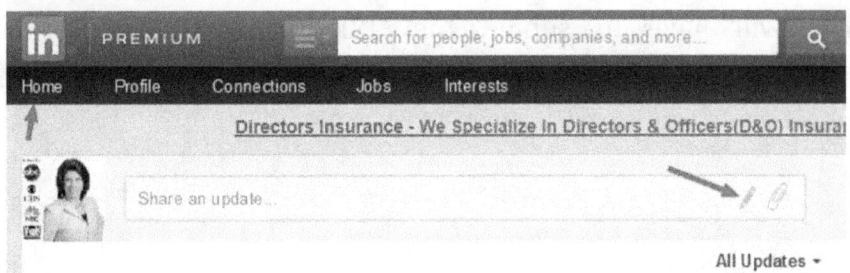

Click the pencil and you'll go to a "compose" screen. This is where you add your text, images and links. To prevent the risk of publishing something before you're ready, or accidentally deleting your hard work, I recommend that you write and edit your piece in a Word document and then paste it into this screen.

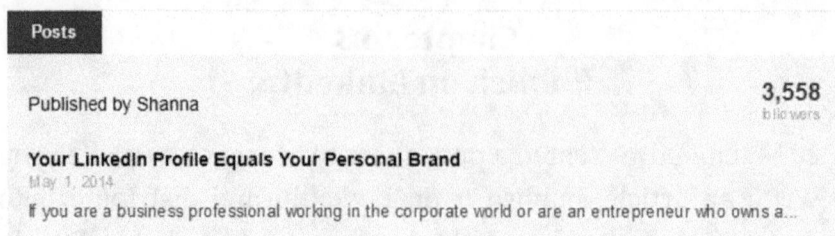

If you don't wish to publish, but do want to have a great status update that gets noticed, you can now attach files, videos, photos, and documents to your status posts. Just click on the paperclip in the **Share an update...** bar.

If you don't have access to LinkedIn's Publishing Platform and want early access, you can apply here: http://specialedition.linkedin.com/publishing/

You will have to submit the URLs of two examples of professional content that you have written.

Publishing Platform
Apply for early access

We're offering our members a powerful new way to build their professional brand — publishing on LinkedIn. When a member publishes a post on LinkedIn, their original content becomes part of their professional profile, is shared with their trusted network, and has the ability to reach the world's largest group of professionals.

We'll be steadily expanding this feature to all members in multiple languages. In the meantime, if you're interested in participating, please fill out the form below.

First name

Shanna

Last name

Landolt

LinkedIn public profile URL

http://www.linkedin.com/in/shannalandolt

You will find this on your profile

[in] www.linkedin.com/in/johndoe/

Email

Examples of professional content you have written

URL of first example

URL of second example

Apply

Chapter 14
Basic Free Account or Premium Account

Most LinkedIn Users have the basic free account. According to Statista.com 84.4% of LinkedIn Users use the free account, 15.1% use the paid account and 0.5% aren't sure. [1]

Free LinkedIn account usage among members as of May 2014

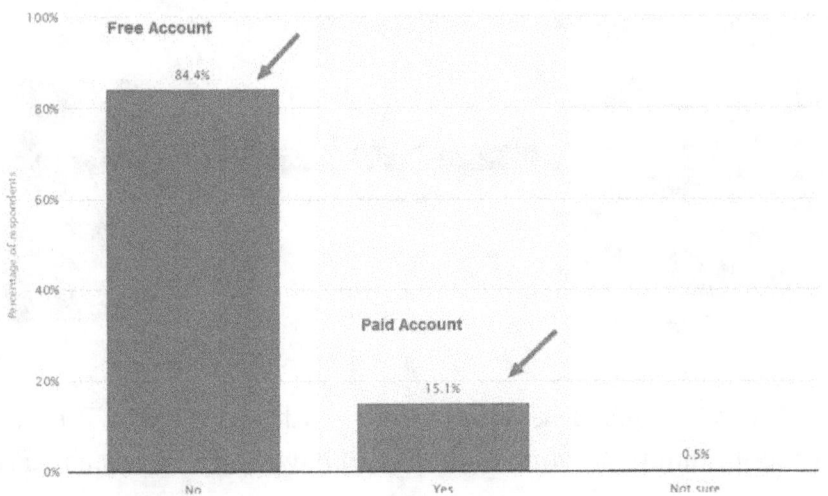

Before June 2014 I would have told you that the basic, free account was fine. However, I may have just changed my mind about that. In June 2014 LinkedIn added some new features to their Premium Account that make you look *great*. If you are active in a job search or use LinkedIn for business development, I would definitely suggest a Premium Account. You should also use the Premium account if you are actively creating your personal brand using LinkedIn.

Premium account holders have a larger photo with a background image. LinkedIn has uploaded some background templates that you can use, or you can create a custom background of your own. You can use a JPG, PNG, or GIF under 4MB in size. A resolution of

1400 by 425 pixels looks best.

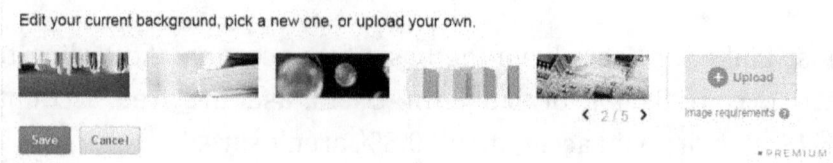

Here's an example of what your profile can look like with a background image.

Currently LinkedIn is testing this with only their Premium account holders. If you would like to have early access as a Free account holder, you can go to: http://specialedition.linkedin.com/custom-backgrounds and sign up for early access.

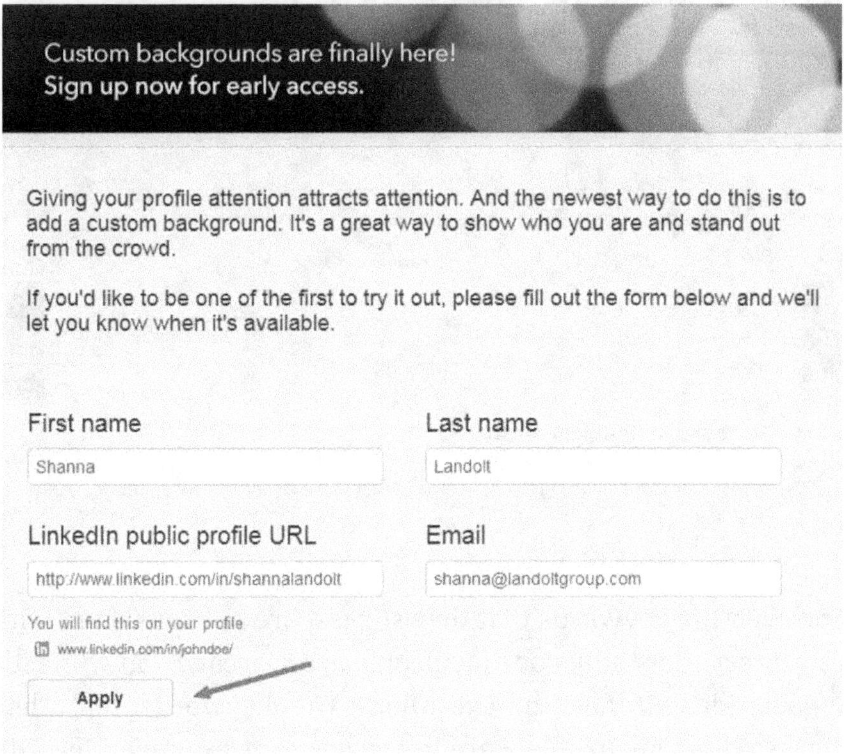

Secrets from a Headhunter

Custom backgrounds are finally here!
Sign up now for early access.

Giving your profile attention attracts attention. And the newest way to do this is to add a custom background. It's a great way to show who you are and stand out from the crowd.

If you'd like to be one of the first to try it out, please fill out the form below and we'll let you know when it's available.

First name

Shanna

Last name

Landolt

LinkedIn public profile URL

http://www.linkedin.com/in/shannalandolt

Email

shanna@landoltgroup.com

You will find this on your profile
www.linkedin.com/in/johndoe/

Apply

Your profile also gets a 2x larger listing space on search results.

Understanding how important the right keywords are to being found on LinkedIn, they now provide keyword suggestions when you start to edit your profile.

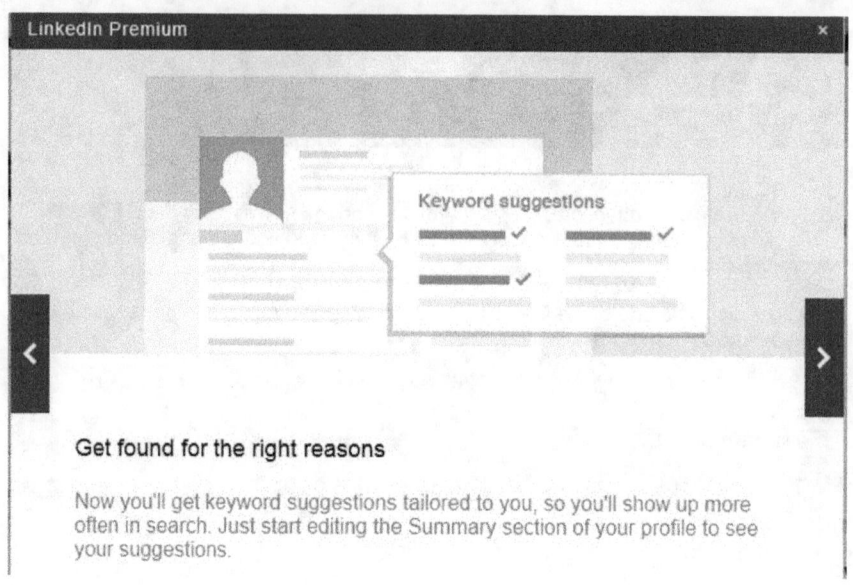

Get found for the right reasons

Now you'll get keyword suggestions tailored to you, so you'll show up more often in search. Just start editing the Summary section of your profile to see your suggestions.

However, the keywords that they suggest are not consistent with how a recruiter thinks or how people are searched. So while it's a good idea, it fails in execution. The keywords that they suggested for my profile were irrelevant. For example LinkedIn suggested the keywords "Candidates alike" and "Based on client". No one will search for those terms in a keyword search.

If you are interested in "How you rank", you can see how your profile compares to your connections or colleagues for profile views. What would be more relevant though is to track how you compare to people with similar experience or job titles.

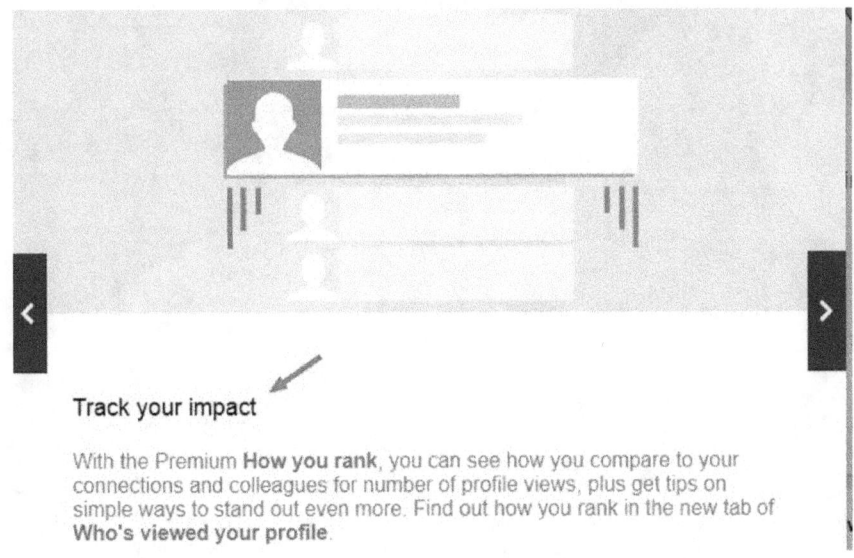

Track your impact

With the Premium **How you rank**, you can see how you compare to your connections and colleagues for number of profile views, plus get tips on simple ways to stand out even more. Find out how you rank in the new tab of **Who's viewed your profile**.

What is interesting here is it also makes it easy to see your total number of connections.

You rank in the top 4% for profile views among your connections.

#135 out of 3,560   ▼ 1% in the last 7 days

Finally, with a Premium Account you get to see the full list of who's viewed your profile, which is incredibly useful. You can contact anyone with InMail. And, you can see expanded profiles.

It's also my opinion that LinkedIn will soon start to charge for some of the features that are currently free in LinkedIn. LinkedIn is interesting because if you aren't paying for the product, by default you ARE the product!

Chapter 15
Cool Tools and Apps to Get the Most Out of LinkedIn

There are a lot of great third-party apps that can be combined to with LinkedIn to really optimize the experience and get the most out of the platform. I'll run through some of my favourites below.[1]

Wordle™ <u>http://www</u>.wordle.net

1. Wordle generates "word clouds" from text that you provide, which can really help your keyword research. The clouds give greater prominence to words that appear more frequently in the source text. Cut and Paste sample job descriptions of jobs that you are interested in into Wordle. You will then see which words appear most frequently in those documents. Go back to your LinkedIn Profile (and your resume) and drop in those words in appropriate places so that your profile will read as a great match for the job.

<u>http://www</u>.sync.me

2. Sync.me Integrates your Phone contacts with Facebook, LinkedIn and Google+. Sync.me seamlessly updates your Contacts with their latest pictures and information. If someone updates or changes something on their profile, for example, their job title, Sync.me automatically updates that information in your phone contacts.

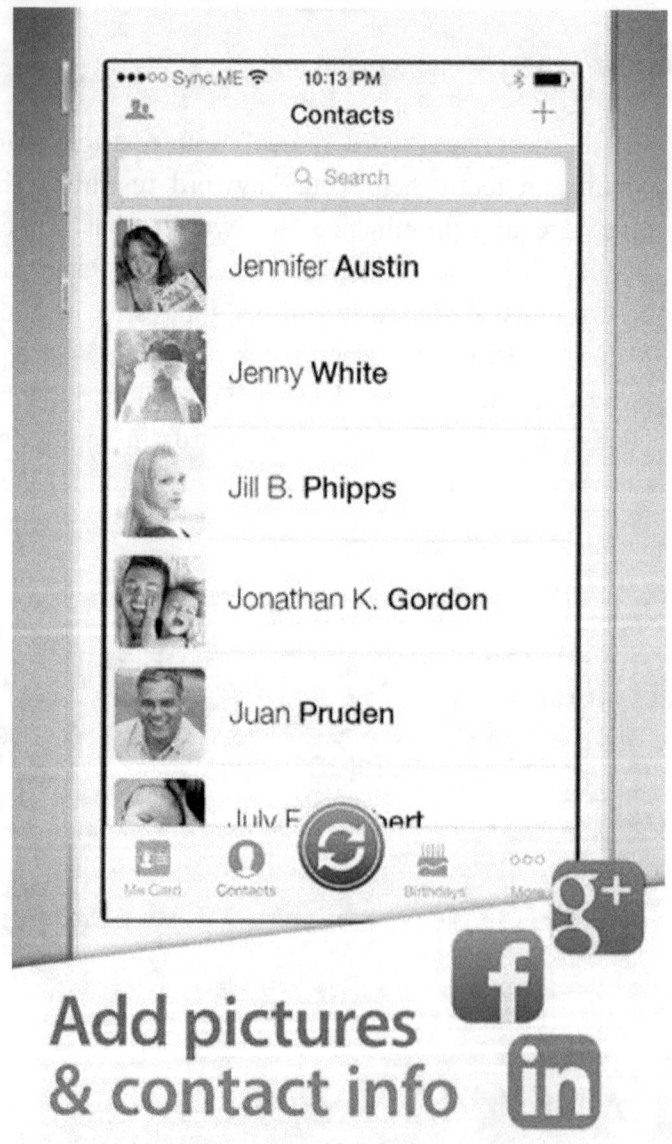

FIVEHUNDREDPLUS www.fivehundredplus.com

3. Use FiveHundredPlus to choose your most important connections from LinkedIn and schedule when you would like to reach out to them. Simply drag them to the appropriate column: Weekly, Monthly, Quarterly or Yearly. Every Monday, Five Hundred Plus will send you an e-mail with that week's connections for you to follow up with. They will colour those connections in red if you are overdue. It's like having a mini CRM system.

 http://tinyurl.com/82swucc

4. Microsoft Office Social Connector synchronizes your LinkedIn contact data with Outlook. Within Outlook, you can stay up to date on the status and activities of your contacts, whether they are from your organization's network, or from social networking sites on the Internet.

OR If you use Gmail

www.rapportive.com

Rapportive is an add on to Gmail. When you are corresponding with someone in your Gmail, Rapportive will look check LinkedIn to find details on the person. Rapportive allows you to automatically see who they are, what their background is and also connect to them on LinkedIn if you are not already connected.

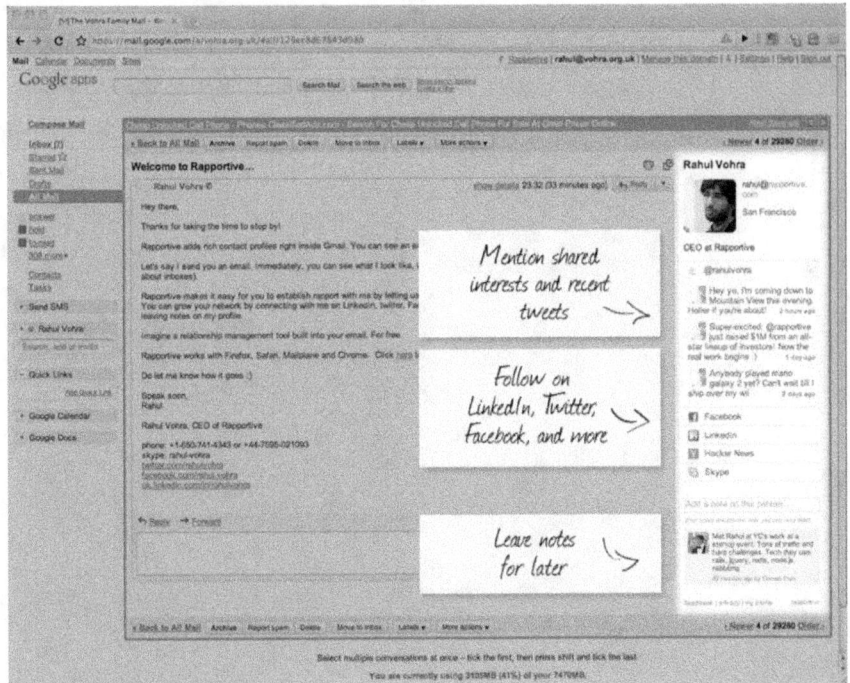

 www.oktopost.com

5. Use Oktopost to schedule posts on LinkedIn. You can upload photos, share and automatically shorten links, post to multiple LinkedIn groups, post on different tabs, automatically save and re-use content and much more. It's the easiest way to schedule a discussion across your entire group set. You can schedule a post on 50 different LinkedIn groups in less than 30 seconds.

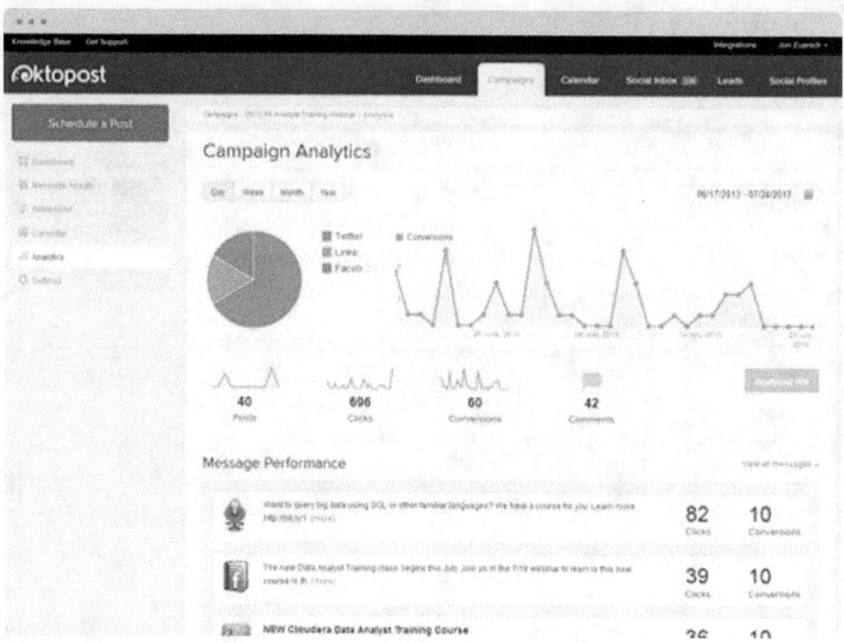

LunchMeet www.lunchmeetapp.com

6. The LunchMeet app allows for you to network whenever you are available. It's a great tool for talent hunters, job seekers, career development professionals, recruiters, entrepreneurs, people who seek free consultation over lunch/drinks, business school students, business development/sales/marketing people, and anyone who is interested in strengthening and expanding their professional network.

Here's how it works:

- Sign-in with your LinkedIn account (necessary)

- Let the app know when you will be available to meet and where

- Search for other professionals in your area who are also available within the same timeslot

- Invite them to a LunchMeet!

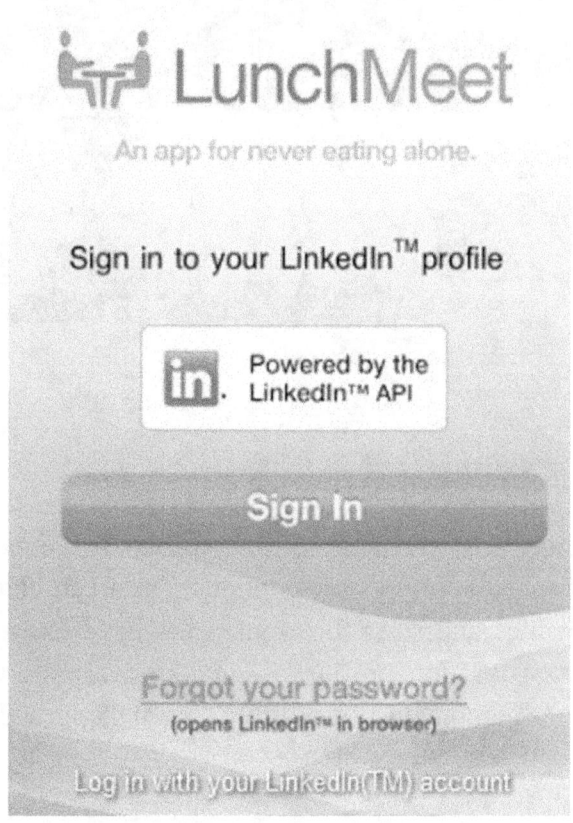

SlideShare. www.slideshare.net

7. SlideShare is presentation tool owned by LinkedIn and it's an easy way to share your expertise. You can create webinars, embed YouTube videos, upload sales or marketing presentations, portfolios, and PDFs. You connect to it through LinkedIn and then embed your presentations to broadcast your expertise and thought leadership.

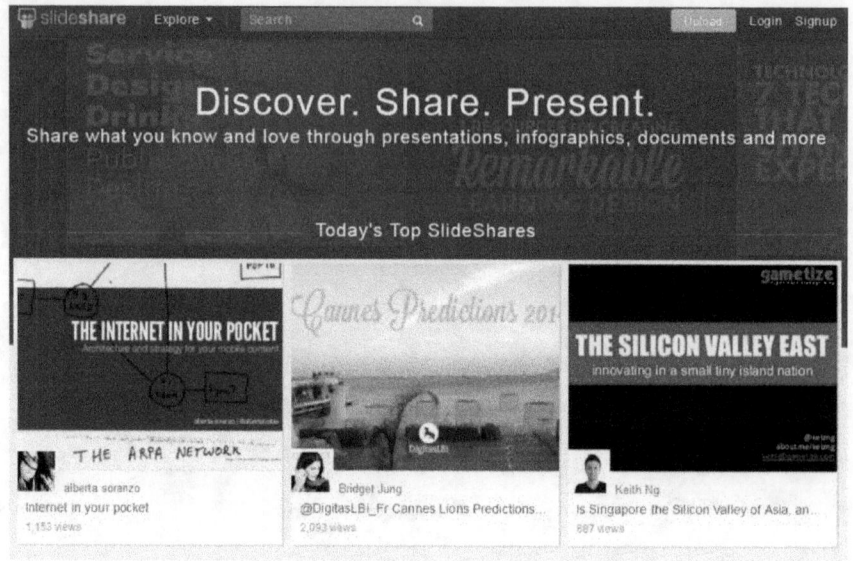

OFunnel www.ofunnel.com

8. OFunnel lets you choose what LinkedIn connections you want to be kept up to date about. You can choose similar companies and roles that your peers have chosen based on industry, location, profile data, and other signals. Once a day, OFunnel automatically tells you what happened with your connections.

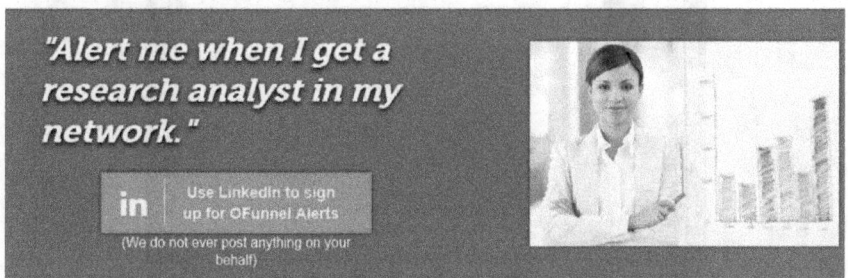

Google Alerts for Relationships.

OFunnel delivers the most relevant connections within your expanding network.

No more noise. No more missing out when connections happen.

Evernote www.evernote.com

9. Evernote allows you to automatically build a content-rich note around every business card you scan with your iPhone or iPad (and soon for Android). It includes full contact information, a link to their current LinkedIn profile, and a photo, plus a section for notes. Business cards become searchable contacts in Evernote. You don't have to be connected with the person on LinkedIn for this to work.

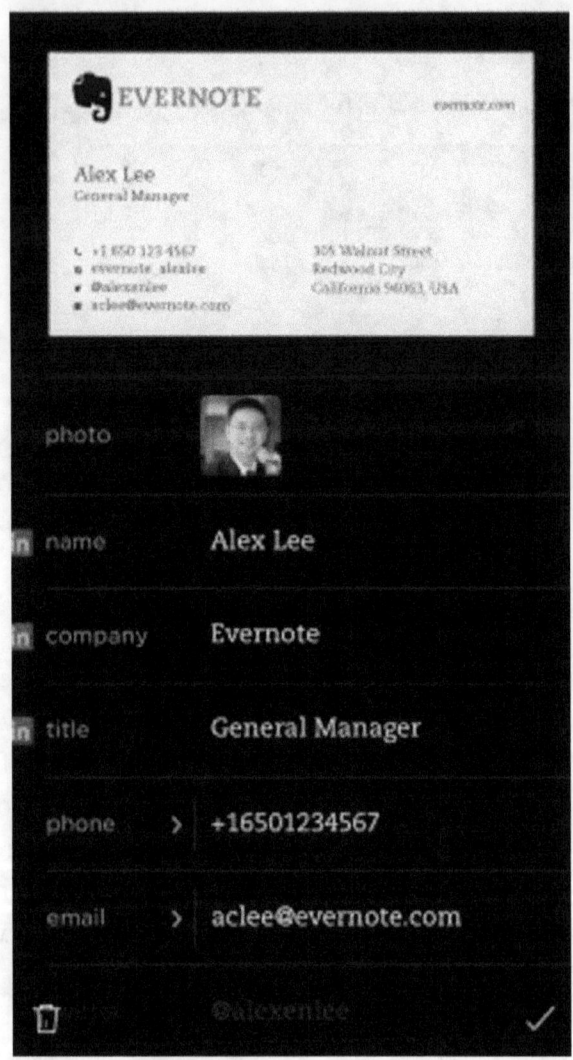

Wordpress WORDPRESS www.wordpress.com

10. You can add your blog to LinkedIn using Wordpress. If

you blog, you simply *must* link your Blog to LinkedIn. Here is the link to do it! http://wordpress.org/plugins/wp-linkedin/

Also, here is a guide with instructions for how to connect your WordPress.com blog. http://en.support.wordpress.com/publicize/

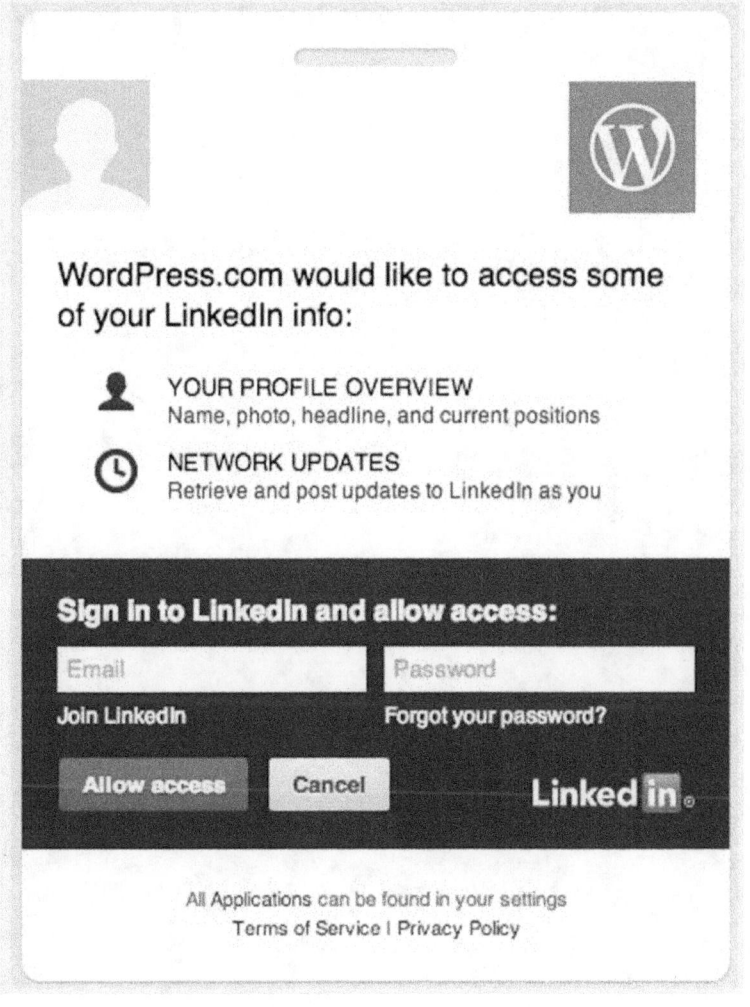

Chapter 16
LinkedIn's Apps

LinkedIn itself offers 4 Apps you may find useful. Here are the highlights[1]...

1. LinkedIn for Smart Phones:

Mobile now represents more than 40% of traffic to LinkedIn[2], so it's a good idea to make sure that you have the most current version of this software for your device.

Once it's installed, go to the LinkedIn app on your phone and check your settings. On your iPhone app: Look for the gear ⚙ in the upper right corner and review the settings.

If you click on the LinkedIn logo at the top left corner, then click on the paper+pencil icon at the top right corner, it pops up three customization choices: New Message, New Invitation, Cancel.

I don't recommend connecting with people on your phone. You can't personalize your requests. If you are on someone's profile and hit Connect, LinkedIn will just send an automatic invitation. These are impersonal. If the person doesn't know who you are or why you are sending the request, they may delete it or report it as a SPAM message.

However, I do find the phone app incredibly handy when I'm waiting for a meeting and want to quickly look someone up.

If you sync your phone's calendar with LinkedIn's app, you will get the profile of anyone you have pencilled in on your schedule. It makes it easy to refresh yourself about their background before you meet so that you are prepared. I LOVE this feature!

Select "Calendar" from the list of options in the app's menu bar and follow the instructions.

From the app's menu you can follow specific companies. LinkedIn will provide a list of recommendations. Once you follow a company, LinkedIn will call up its profile in the Companies tab. Then you can browse a company's page; see their updates, employees, and job postings. The Companies tab is a one stop destination for all the news about any company you are interested in. Also, once you are following a company, its updates and any content that it shares will also show up in your news stream.

You can apply for jobs directly through LinkedIn's app. The list of positions in the "Jobs" section are tailored to your interests and are customized from your own LinkedIn data. You can apply for a position just by submitting your profile. NOTE – *I don't recommend that you do this but it's cool to know that you can.* ☺

You can use your news stream to build your personal brand and to strengthen your connections. You can "like" and comment on almost every kind of post. You can congratulate someone who got a new job, or comment or share an article. Remember that the comments on LinkedIn are for a business audience. Put some thought into what you post.

2. LinkedIn iPad

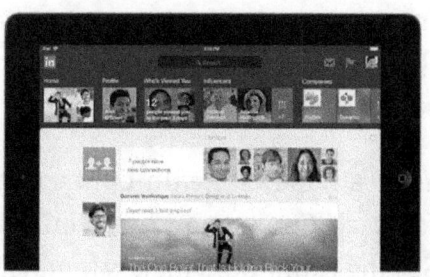

LinkedIn for iPad

All the opportunity you need in one big, beautiful feed. Keep refreshing what you know with the latest industry news, influencer insights, and updates from your network. If you're not tapping in, you're missing out.

Once you've installed the app on your iPad, look for your LinkedIn profile photo on the far right, click and choose Settings. The settings and navigation on the iPad are not the same as the settings on the iPhone. The boxes across the top (keep scrolling to the right) show the various LinkedIn sections available including: Home, Profile, Connections, Influencers, Groups, Companies, Who's Viewed You, Jobs, People You May Know, and Channels.

3. LinkedIn Contacts www.linkedin.com/contacts

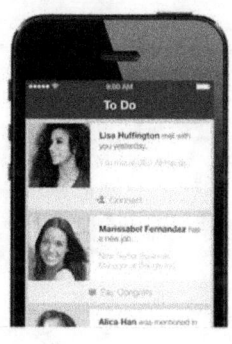

Contacts

Never miss an opportunity to say hello. All of your contact information together in one helpful app. With job change and birthday alerts, and easily accessible relationship history that's available at a moment's (or meeting's) notice, it's a smarter way to stay in touch.

The LinkedIn Contacts app is a completely separate app from the LinkedIn mobile app. You can use it on your laptop, desktop or smart phone. It connects your calendar of events, keeps track of recent conversations, informs you of changes in your connections' world, and allows you to stay in touch more easily. LinkedIn Contacts is like a mini CRM where you can easily manage your relationships. You can call your contacts directly from this app. If your contact has listed their phone number in their LinkedIn profile, you can call straight from the app. The same goes for e-mailing them.

You can use LinkedIn Contacts to take notes and set reminders for each Connection that you are trying to stay in contact with. Setting reminders makes it much easier for you to follow up.

Go to your desktop or laptop and download LinkedIn Contacts. Then sync your e-mail and calendars. You can sync with Outlook, Gmail, Google+, Yahoo, Facebook, Twitter, Evernote and Tripit.

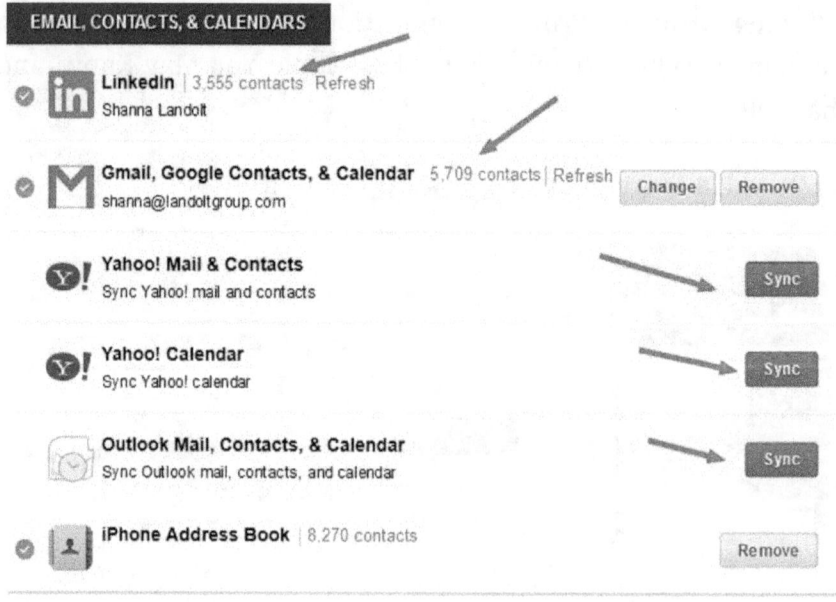

Syncing your contact information helps you to keep in touch with your connections. When you sync your e-mail it will reference your e-mail history so you can see the sender and subject line of each of your recent messages.

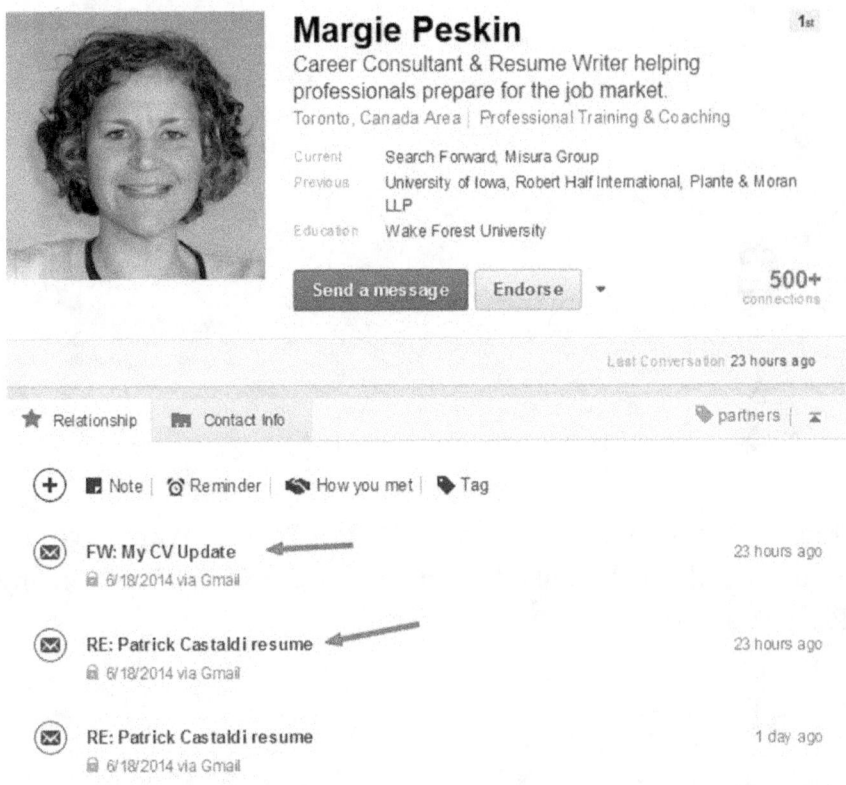

LinkedIn updates this daily. When you sync your calendar, you also get to see your meeting history with people. LinkedIn Contacts will tell you who is in your next meeting in case you haven't connected. This gets updated daily.

You can also filter your contacts by: All Contacts, Connections Only, Company, Tag, Location, Title, Source, Saved, Hidden and Potential duplicates.

Clint Arthur is one of my contacts and I can see that we are connected through LinkedIn and Gmail and he is also in my iPhone Contacts.

4. LinkedIn Pulse

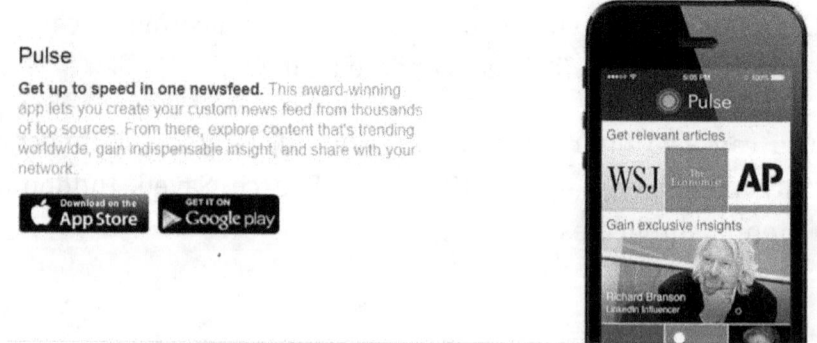

LinkedIn acquired Pulse for $90 Million, so they are really serious about this app. You can open the LinkedIn Pulse tab to see a selection of articles and news about topics related to who you follow and your industry. It's easy to share these articles to your LinkedIn Profile as well as to other Social Media like Facebook, Google+, or Twitter. You can sort by Your News, Top Posts, All Influences, All Channels, and All Publishers. The content here is GREAT!

Pulse has hundreds of content partnerships with publishers that enabled Pulse to serve up a majority of or all of a publisher's content directly within their app. Executives are now turning to LinkedIn Pulse as a major source of news specifically because it is so easy to share and contribute great articles to your network. If you are active in a job search, sharing relevant articles is a great strategy for staying top-of-mind, while completely avoiding sounding pushy or desperate. But be discerning in what you share — go for quality over quantity!

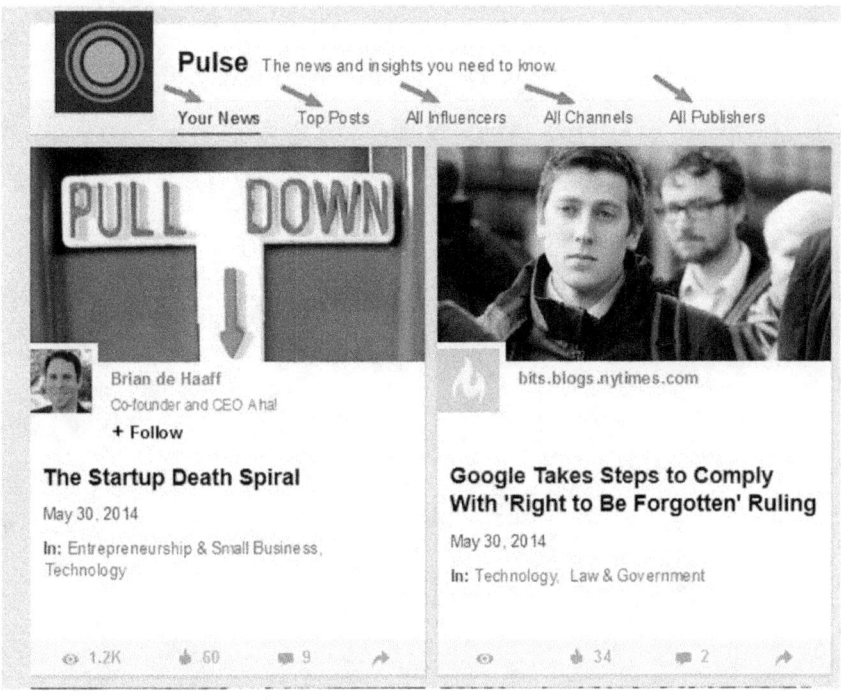

Conclusion

Congratulations on taking the time to read this book. If you implement the strategies I've recommended and have the right connections and keywords, your LinkedIn Profile will be a great tool in developing your personal brand, building your network, and attracting the right opportunities. Your profile will be in the top 1% on LinkedIn.

If you have technical questions about LinkedIn, the best place to go is: http://community.linkedin.com/questions/ask.html. This is a community online forum where the questions and answers are public.

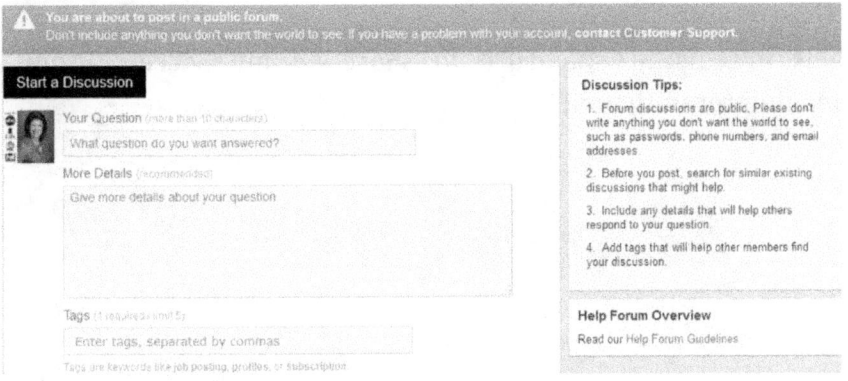

Remember that LinkedIn changes all the time. If you would like to sign up for up-to-date articles about LinkedIn best practices and Career Advice, go to www.secretsfromaheadhunter.com

I also invite you to connect with me personally at ca.linkedin.com/in/shannalandolt

I hope you've enjoyed Secrets From a Headhunter: LinkedIn for Pharmaceutical & Biotechnology Professionals. Please share a review on Amazon!

If you have a question about LinkedIn that wasn't in this edition of the book, please e-mail me at shanna@landoltgroup.com. I'll answer your question and may even add it to the next edition!

"Like" our Facebook Fan page now https://www.facebook.com/secretsfromaheadhunter to connect with other readers and receive additional LinkedIn and Job Search tips and advice.

I invite you to join the Secrets From a Headhunter group on LinkedIn at

http://www.linkedin.com/groups?home=&gid=8127803   You can network and share job tips and advice in this group.

It is my distinct pleasure to share all my Secrets From a Headhunter with you!

About the Author

As Seen On...

Shanna Landolt is the President of Secrets From a Headhunter and The Landolt Group, a Toronto-based Executive Search firm that specializes in recruiting executives in the pharmaceutical and biotechnology industry. She has more than 15 years of recruitment experience and has interviewed thousands of candidates and placed hundreds of people in six-figure jobs.

Shanna has been featured in the news and on morning talk shows as a LinkedIn and Hiring expert on NBC, FOX, CityTV, and the Life Network. She has been cited by ABC and CBS as a LinkedIn Authority.

She is a contributing author, along with Brian Tracy and Tom Hopkins, to the book "101 Great Ways to Compete in Today's Job Market". She is committed to people loving their lives and going to work each day doing something they are passionate about. Clients consider her a trusted adviser.

The Landolt Group
2 Bloor Street East, Suite 3500
Toronto, ON
M4W 1A8
416-849-3855

Shanna is an OpenLink Networker on LinkedIn
Connect with her at:

ca.linkedin.com/in/shannalandolt

shanna@landoltgroup.com

More From This Author

If you would like to learn more about Secrets From a Headhunter and our Services, go to www.secretsfromaheadhunter.com You'll also find some great free downloads including a LinkedIn Checklist. Here's to your success!

To learn more about The Landolt Group and our services go to www.landoltgroup.com

Thank You!

I want to thank my husband, Paul Landolt for all of his technical expertise. And thanks for being patient while I spent all those hours up in my office writing in the evenings. I love you honey!

A special thank you to Aaron Sugarman for your work in helping to edit this book. Aaron Sugarman and his wife Caroline Sugarman are fabulous coaches at WYSIWYGco Coaching. Thank you for continually taking "just one more request for your opinion".

Thank you to Clint Arthur who got me to realize that I had a unique positioning as both a recruiter and a LinkedIn Expert!

And thank you to the folks at GKIC, Expert Catapult and Lisa Sasevich's Speak-to-Sell who inspired me to write this book.

Finally, to my beautiful children Brooke, Karrington, and Hayden. I love you! You inspire me to continually reinvent myself so we have the opportunity to live an exceptional life as a family.

And to everyone who reads this book – I wish you LinkedIn Success and the career of your dreams.

One Last Thing...

Amazon will give you the opportunity to rate this book and share your thoughts on Facebook and Twitter. If you believe the book is worth sharing, would you please take a few seconds to let your friends know about it?

Here's to Your Success!

Shanna Landolt

End Notes

---

[1] http://expandedramblings.com/index.php/by-the-numbers-a-few-important-linkedin-stats/

[1] http://help.linkedin.com/app/answers/detail/a_id/4447/~/linkedin-search-relevance---people-search

[2] http://blog.sironaconsulting.com/sironasays/2012/08/this-is-why-your-linkedin-profile-is-not-showing-up-in-peoples-linkedin-searches.html

[3] http://www.linkedin.com/static?key=pop%2Fpop_more_profile_completeness

[4] http://www.linkedin.com/static?key=pop%2Fpop_more_profile_completeness

[5] http://community.linkedin.com/questions/4568/maximum-characters-counts-for-2013.html

[1] http://blog.linkedin.com/2014/02/24/making-it-easier-to-manage-your-professional-identity-on-linkedin/

[2] http://help.linkedin.com/app/answers/detail/a_id/1615/~/adding-or-changing-your-profile-photo

[3] http://help.linkedin.com/app/answers/detail/a_id/430/related/1

[4] Photo Credit : www.PhotoByAzi.com

[1] http://blog.linkedin.com/2013/12/11/buzzwords-2013/

[1] http://www.blogging4jobs.com/social-media/7-things-you-need-to-know-about-linkedin-search

[1] http://www.statista.com/statistics/264074/percentage-of-paying-linkedin-users/

[1] http://socialmediatoday.com/pamdyer/2204606/8-linkedin-tools-business

[1] https://www.linkedin.com/mobile

[2] http://investors.linkedin.com/releasedetail.cfm?ReleaseID=823992

www.ingramcontent.com/pod-product-compliance
Lightning Source LLC
Chambersburg PA
CBHW051512170526
45166CB00001B/492